❖❖❖ SUPERHINTS ❖❖❖

Compiled by
the Lady Wardington

With a foreword by
His Grace the Duke of Marlborough

Michael Joseph
London

Michael Joseph Ltd

Published by the Penguin Group
27 Wrights Lane, London W8 5TZ, England
Viking Penguin Inc., 375 HudsonStreet, New York 10014, USA
Penguin Books Australia Ltd, Ringwood, Victoria, Australia
Penguin Books Canada Ltd, 10 Alcorn Avenue, Ontario,
Canada, M4V 3B2
Penguin Books (NZ) Ltd, 182-190 Wairau Road, Auckland 10, New
Zealand
Penguin Books Ltd, Registered Offices: Harmondsworth, Middlesex,
England

First published in Great Britain 1991
Second impression November 1991
Third impression December 1991
Fourth impression December 1991
Fifth impression October 1992

All royalties from this book are to be donated to
the Katharine House Hospice Trust, Aynho Road, Adderbury, Banbury,
Oxfordshire.

Printed and bound in Great Britain by Butler and Tanner Ltd
Frome and London
Design and computer make-up by Penny Mills

A CIP catalogue record for this book is available from the
British Library

ISBN O 7181 3505 9

The hints in this book are intended to suggest possible
solutions only. While every effort has been made to check
their accuracy, the compiler, contributors and publisher
can neither guarantee absolute success nor accept any legal
responsibility or liability for their effectiveness.

❖❖❖ Contents ❖❖❖

FOREWORD

Like many words in our language the word 'hospice' has often changed its meaning. For a thousand years it described a stopping place for pilgrims, some of whom would arrive ill or injured and would in fact die there, though most would continue on their way. Since the turn of the century a hospice has come to mean a worldwide movement for developing skills and, just as important, attitudes needed in caring for the terminally ill.

For example, every year in this country 130,000 people die of cancer. That is 20 per cent of all deaths. Many are elderly, many are young, some are even children. The process of dying and the practical and emotional problems associated with it place a heavy burden on the individual and the family. So all cancer patients need the best possible care during the last weeks or months of their lives. The hospice movement aims to provide that care through specially trained doctors, nurses, social workers and others working with dedication and love.

Hospice care is based on a simple philosophy: that a dying person is a living person who needs dignity, security and calm in that final period. Hospice care aims to control pain and other depressing symptoms; it tries to meet personal, emotional and spiritual needs; and it offers support to relatives both during the illness and in bereavement. In the words of one hospice doctor: 'We want to make the patient's body a comfortable place to live in. Then he is free, if he wishes, to prepare for death mentally and spiritually.'

In 1984 two groups of people – one professionally concerned, the other suffering from personal loss – met in Banbury. They met because they shared the hospice movement's philosophy and because they perceived the need for enhanced provision for the 300–350 local people who die of malignant diseases each year.

Inevitably, because of their shared aims, the two groups joined forces in January 1985 as the Katharine House Hospice Trust, taking the name of a young student, Katharine Gadsby, who died of cancer at the age of twenty, as a symbol of all those who need care and as a reminder that the illness is no respecter of age.

Katharine House is now established and is offering care to members of the community. It exists and will continue to exist because of the generosity and concern of everyone.

Marlborough.

INTRODUCTION

The fascination of this book is that it is not just another catalogue of anonymous tips. Refreshingly, it is a collection of ideas contributed by people from all walks of life who have found, through trial and error, that they really do work, on subjects as diverse, colourful and interesting as they are themselves.

Princess Margaret's way of removing wine stains from the carpet, Paul Eddington's method of cleaning brass and Mrs Thatcher's approach to bridging awkward time-zones all have the credibility of personal experience. And did you know – I didn't – that you can cook soufflés straight from the freezer, catch a horse by walking away from it, ward off greenfly with garlic, or 'cork' an opened bottle of champagne with a silver teaspoon?

Although many people diffidently thought that their hints were old hat and known to everyone, to me, an old hint collector, almost all were new. Sadly there was not room in the book to include every hint received; and where several people sent the same hint only one version has been included. To everyone who took the time and the trouble to share their personal favourites, I give my heartfelt thanks.

Without the help of Laurie Purden I could not have even started out on this project. Not only did she gather a great many of the hints, but she made sure they were in proper order and understandable. The fact that we are still on speaking terms says a great deal for her sense of humour and patience and I am eternally grateful to her.

For me, compiling the entries has been a labour of love. It so happened that Marion Shaw, my secretary and close friend of many years, was being cared for in a hospice at the very time I became involved in raising funds for the building of Katharine House, to which all the proceeds of this book will go. Her end, surrounded by the loving care that such places provide, was this book's beginning.

Audrey Waddington

TRAVELLING

The only way to be sure of catching a train is to miss the one before it.

G. K. CHESTERTON

GO FOR A DISCOUNT

You can often do a better deal with a hotel if you book it yourself rather than through a travel agent – after all, he gets a commission. The best way is to start negotiations a couple of months before-hand, communicate by fax and offer to pay for at least the first night in advance.

H H Judge Fox-Andrews

CHECK YOUR TICKETS

It sounds obvious, but you should always check your tickets when you receive them. Travel agents are only human and can book seats on the wrong day – I know, because it's happened to me!

The Lord Wardington

A HEAD START

Problem: Your regular stylist has got your hair looking just the way you want it. But you're off on a business trip/holiday abroad and know from bitter experience how difficult it is to get unknown hairdressers to follow suit.

Solution: Get someone (your own hairdresser or a friend) to take photographs – front, back and sides – of your hair the way you like it and take them with you.

Nicky Smith
Author of The Style of an Englishman

LIST IT

When you're unpacking your suitcase there always seems to be one important thing that's been forgotten – often many more. Make a careful list on a 6" x 4" card; keep it in a well-remembered place, and before each trip tick off every item.

The Viscountess Eccles

HIS AND HERS

Airlines have been known to lose suitcases – it is really a wonder that they don't lose more. It you travel with a companion it's a good idea to pack half-and-half. If each of you have clothes in both suitcases, and one strays, at least you have something to wear until it turns up.

Mrs T. Kimball Brooker

READY, STEADY, GO

I always keep a wash-bag ready packed and prepared for quick trips. I have duplicates of all my creams and lotions and shampoos in *little* bottles with a toothbrush and tiny toothpaste so that I'm ready to go. I also do this with make-up. One bag is full of duplicates, ready to grab. If you use tiny bottles of everything it makes it very light to carry.

Fiona Fullerton
Actress

SEPARATE SUITCASES

As I travel extensively, I always pack my toiletries, shoes and hair things in a separate bag so that they are easily accessible on arrival at my destination, and I don't have to unpack the main suitcase to retrieve them.

Barbara Daly
Make-up artist

A GREAT PACKING METHOD

Because I used to get exasperated at opening a suitcase of crumpled clothes, however carefully I had packed, I have come up with what I think is a great packing method. Lay out all the things that you know will crush horribly, and then pack all the indestructible things like T-shirts, bras, tights, jeans, etc. inside them, using them as you would tissue paper. It really works.

Nanette Newman
Actress and author

ROLY-POLY

Man-made fibres are much less likely to crease if you roll rather than fold them.

Mrs Brian Henderson

PROTECTING THE PLEATS

A pleated skirt will travel beautifully if you roll it into a cylinder shape and insert it by the waistband into the toe of a stocking. Pull the stocking over the skirt so that it looks like a tube and lay this along the back of your suitcase.

Dulcie Gray
Actress and author

CREASE-FREE

Clothes should be packed on lightweight hangers in polythene bags. On arrival, remove polythene and shake.

Caroline Charles
Fashion designer

IN THE BAG

I always pack an extra carry-bag – one of those soft, very light nylon ones that folds up into nothing – to hold the holiday washing I don't get time to launder. It starts out empty, of course, and fills up as I go along. But it is still very light to carry – and so much more pleasant than having dirty things jumbled up with the clean ones in your suitcase.

The worst thing about moving around a lot is having so little time to organize personal bits and pieces. I've learned to segregate, packing everything – jewellery, tights, make-up, sun-creams, even belts – into separate containers. But instead of those nasty plastic ones, I buy Liberty print bags in the sale. They squidge up into the corners of your suitcase, and lift out easily when you arrive. They lift the spirits, too, by looking so pretty.

Anne Gregg
Travel writer and TV presenter

HOLIDAY HAIR

Don't waste space packing a whole wardrobe of hair combs. All you need is one pair, and a selection of narrow ribbons. Choose the colour you want and, weaving the ribbon up and over between the teeth, wrap it tightly round the shank of the comb until it is completely covered.

Douglas von Katzer
The Bute Street Salon

SUN SHIRT

When you are travelling to the tropics, take an old long-sleeved shirt, preferably white, cotton, man's, and jolly well wear it when you're swimming – at least for the first two days – to protect your arms and shoulders from the blazing sun.

The Lord Glenconner

PRESENTS TO AFRICA

When you are travelling in Third World countries, take lots of cheap, bright biros. Children beg for them – in fact are in dire need of them – and they're much better for them than sweets.

Carol Wright
Travel correspondent, House and Garden

ROLL-UP ADDRESS BOOK

Speed the despatch of postcards when you're travelling around by writing out all the names and addresses on a roll of small adhesive labels before you go. The roll will fit neatly into the smallest corner of your suitcase and no address book is needed.

Mrs Tony Slater

TALKING PICTURES

Students, particularly in Asian countries, will be very keen to talk to you to practise their English. Take photographs of your family and home with you. They will be a source of great interest and give you lots to talk about.

Manora Simaika
Tour manager

NO BATH PLUG

If you're planning a trip to Eastern Europe, take a bath plug (a squash ball serves equally well) as hotels are very often without them.

Countess Michalowska

EASY IDENTIFICATION

My father, who was a great traveller, used to tie brightly coloured ribbons to the handles of his suitcases so that they were easy to spot in a crowd. That was many years ago, long before you could buy coloured straps for the same purpose, but it's still a good idea.

Patric Walker
Astrologer

FOILED!

Airlines are very keen on having all suitcases labelled, and the thieves who hang around airports love this. All they have to do is read your address and then, knowing you will be away, nip round to your house and 'do' it in peace. Foil them by putting your destination address on the *outside* of the case and your home address on a sticky label *inside*.

Audrey Whiting
Journalist

AIRPORT HAVEN

If the airport is overcrowded with long delays, seek peace and calm in the airport chapel, which is usually an oasis of quiet and has plenty of space.

Carol Wright
Travel correspondent, House and Garden

TIME CHANGE

I have learnt to minimize the effects of jet-lag by setting my watch to the time of my destination while I am still on the plane, and then resolutely going to bed at what would be normal at this time (no earlier and no later).

Sir David Attenborough
Broadcaster and naturalist

AVOIDING JET LAG

If you want to avoid jet lag the secret is not to go to sleep when travelling across the time lines but to extend your day until it is night where you are now – even if it means doing nearly thirty-six hours at a stretch without sleep!

The Rt. Hon. Mrs Margaret Thatcher

CLEAN FIZZ

If the person next to you on the aeroplane tips his breakfast over you, and you're wearing a neat outfit to make a good impression on arrival, don't panic. Ask the flight attendant for lots of soda water and soak up the stains with a cloth. By the time you arrive you will be clean and dry!

Moira Shearer
Writer and ballerina

FEET IN A BAG

Members of the Royal Ballet put brown paper bags over their feet on long flights; they say it stops their ankles from swelling.

Mrs John Gorst

BUMPING UP

Though tracksuits are the most comfortable clothes for travelling, if there's a chance you could be upgraded to a better class through overbooking dress neatly and well; airlines won't upgrade those in shorts, T-shirts, jeans and such.

Carol Wright
Travel correspondent, House and Garden

GETTING THERE

Why *is* it that holiday postcards never seem to arrive until after you are home again? My solution is to write them as soon as I arrive, add UK stamps and send them all in a big envelope to an obliging friend, asking her to post them on for me.

June Ducas
Journalist

STEAMED UP

In a hotel, when trying to render crumpled clothes creaseless, turn on the shower (hot) for five minutes with the door closed and then hang up the garments for ten minutes.

The Earl of Lichfield
Photographer

READY RECKONING

To convert centigrade to fahrenheit quickly, double the centigrade and add 32. If the answer's under 60, subtract 1; if over, add 1.

Should you wish to be exact, multiply the centigrade by 9, divide the answer by 5 and add 32. Conversely, to convert fahrenheit to centigrade, subtract 32 from the fahrenheit, divide by 9 and multiply by 5.

Tony Wilson
Department store owner

NO ICE

In countries where it isn't safe to drink the water, never have ice in your drink – unless you have made it yourself from bottled water. Freezing does nothing to the bugs, except preserve them.

Philip Bird
Songwriter

PASSPORTS: LOST, STOLEN OR STRAYED

If you've ever lost your passport on holiday you'll know what a nightmare it is. But in most cases the local consul will be able to issue a new one within twenty-four hours provided that you can give him the number of your passport and a copy of your birth certificate. Now, for complete peace of mind, I always carry a photostat of my birth certificate and a note of my passport number abroad with me.

Mike Harding
Entertainer and adventurer

MY TIME'S MY OWN

On our honeymoon we stayed in a hotel where they served lunch at 12.30 a.m. and dinner at 7.30 p.m., which was too early for us. To solve the problem we simply put our watches on an hour so that we were happily eating with everyone else at a time that suited us better. Lord Oranmore and Brown used to do the same thing shooting on his estate in Galway. He set his clocks so that his guests would not realize how early they were rising. If they wanted to make an appointment to see anyone in the neighbourhood they would be asked if they were on local time or 'the Lord's time'.

The Lady Wardington

NEVER ON A TUESDAY

If after driving through France you plan to end up in Paris, try not to make it a Tuesday. On Tuesdays all the state-owned museums *and* some of the others are closed, so if you want your annual fix of the Mona Lisa you'll have to wait.

The Lady May

X-RAY HAZARD

After a holiday place all your films in a clear plastic bag and keep it in your hand luggage. Before going though the airport X-ray, hand over the bag and in most countries it won't have to go through the machine which can harm fast film.

The Earl of Lichfield
Photographer

MOTORING

Beneath this slab
John Brown is stowed.
He watched the ads
And not the road.

OGDEN NASH

WEAR AND TEAR

Unlikely though it sounds, it's far better to buy a much-used car from a commercial traveller than a little-used car from a stay-at-home. Why? Because, as everyone in the motor trade knows, the greatest wear comes from endless cold starts and lots of short runs.

Felix Kelly
Artist

EXTRA PROTECTION

If you are buying a new car, or replacing the tyres on an old one, you can quite easily have inner tubes fitted under tubeless tyres. This prevents the occasional loss of air through the rim seals that results from hitting kerbs or potholes in the normal course of driving.

Stephen Massey
Christie's New York

HIDDEN CAR KEY

Ever since our three-year-old locked herself in the car with the keys in the ignition I've kept a spare key in a magnetic holder attached to the underside of the mudguard.

The Hon. John Fermor-Hesketh

KEEPING IN TOUCH

If you are a woman who has to drive any distances on her own, especially at night, get a mobile phone. The feeling of security it gives far outweighs the cost.

Christine Goodwill
Estate agent

TAPING YOUR TRIP

If, like me, you're hopeless at map-reading or have no natural sense of direction, plan your route before you start and read the directions into a tape recorder. As I drive along I switch the tape on at every tricky turning and hear myself telling me where to go. Needless to say, I also record the return journey: it doesn't work to play the same tape backwards!

Keith Floyd
TV cook

QUICK CONVERSION

To convert kilometres into miles, divide by 8 and multiply by 5. If your arithmetic is awful and you are travelling fast, divide by 10 and multiply by 7: the answer will be near enough.

The Lord May

A QUESTION OF BALANCE

If you place a small piece of Elastoplast on the bone behind your ears, which controls your balance, you will never feel sick in a car. I have tried this with adults and children for years, always with favourable results. My grandchildren now travel from Hertfordshire to Perth on their way to the north of Scotland, which is over 400 miles, without being in the least sick, as they used to be in the past.

Dame Barbara Cartland
Novelist

BAREFOOT

Driving without shoes helps to keep you awake.

Norman Hudson
Adviser on heritage property

TAPE THE LINES

Wear a piece of Scotch tape placed vertically over your frown lines when driving.

Ann Bellah Copeland

IN THE SPOTLIGHT

Years ago I was advised that if I was driving at night and a car came towards me with headlights undipped, it would be a good idea simply to close one eye until it had gone by – that way I would be left with at least half my vision. It's certainly a better system than closing both eyes!

Michael Aspel
TV presenter

EASY RIDER

Oncoming traffic permitting, it is more comfortable and less of a shock to the suspension to drive over 'sleeping policemen' at an angle.

The Rt. Hon. John Biffen
MP

ADVICE FOR FAST DRIVERS

Overtakers, beware of undertakers.

The Rt. Rev. Mervyn Stockwood

HOT TAKE-AWAYS

Keep your fish and chips or Chinese take-away hot on the way home by wrapping it in foil and putting it under the car bonnet.

Tony Blencowe
Trainee mechanic

WHEEL WISE

Changing a wheel on a dark night is a bad enough experience, but if you find you have lost the nuts when you come to put the wheel back it becomes a nightmare. However, you can safely take one nut from each of the other wheels. Three nuts per wheel are enough to get you home or to a garage if you drive carefully.

Robert Rolandson
Chauffeur

EGG BOUND

An emergency measure if your radiator is leaking badly: break at least six eggs into it and the

scrambled result will certainly get you to a garage –
I know, I've had to do it.

Mrs M. Dormer

TERMINALLY CLEAN

The quickest way to clean the battery terminals of
your car when they are green and messy is to pour
hot water over them. Dry them well afterwards
and wipe them with Vaseline.

Ray Cherry
Master builder

TOP TO BOTTOM

When washing a car start with the roof and work
down. This may sound obvious but the
temptation is to start on the really dirty bits at
the bottom.

Rowan Atkinson
Comic actor

FLY FREE

To clean flies off the windscreen, use toothpaste.
Smear it on with a wet rag, wash it off and polish
the glass with newspaper.

Rosemary, Marchioness of Northampton

REAR VIEW?

If your car has no rear windscreen wiper and you
think it might rain, cut a potato in half and rub
the windscreen well with the cut side. The
rainwater will simply roll away without obscuring
your view.

Alex Leon
Musician

SPORT AND LEISURE

There is nothing – absolutely nothing – half so much worth doing as simply messing about in boats.

The Wind in the Willows
KENNETH GRAHAME

EVERY TIME A WINNER

My absolutely infallible way of selecting racehorse winners is to place the list of runners in front of me and incant, 'Dear Mr Skinner, please give me a winner'. You move down the list ticking one horse with each word incanted. You then go down the list incanting the alphabet. When the first letter of the horse's name coincides with the letter of the alphabet pronounced, that is the horse that will win. It got me out of a lot of trouble on the last day at Goodwood.

Derek Nimmo
Actor

NICE TO BE NEAR

Don't even think about putting your nose near your teenage son's trainers – but after a generous sprinkling of bicarbonate of soda inside them last thing at night, they will be sweet as nuts in the morning.

The Hon. Mrs Petrie

SMASH HITS

For the cleanest tennis shoes on court, after a quick scrub to get rid of any dirt on the undersole, wash them in the washing machine on the towel wash – *with* the towels! Out they come, not only very clean, but also smelling sweet.

Camilla della Gherardesca

BOUNCE

Revive old tennis balls by giving them a whirl in the tumbledrier on the warm cycle.

Mrs Anthony Hopkins

ON THE BALL

To plump up dented ping-pong balls, put them in a pan of cold water and bring to the boil. The balls will expand and the dents will disappear.

Mrs Gerhard Bülle

QUICK ON THE DRAW

At a shoot, at the beginning of a drive, vigorously shake your cartridge bag. This will cause the metal ends of the cartridge cases to come uppermost, thus enabling you to load faster.

The Earl of Lichfield
Photographer

BOAT PEOPLE

If you are asked to spend the weekend on a boat, don't arrive with a hard suitcase. Experienced boat people pack in the sort of case that you can hang your clothes in and roll up for carrying. They usually have pockets as well, so when you get to the boat you really don't need to unpack at all – just hang your case up.

The Hon. William Pease
Ear, nose and throat surgeon

CLEAR SIGNALS

Signal flags can be difficult to store, and on a small boat it isn't always easy to find a suitable space to keep them. If you cut six-inch lengths of drainpipe in whichever widths you want, you can stick the lengths together in whatever shapes you need to fit any convenient corner. Label each clearly with the initial of each flag with Dynamo so that they are always easily identifiable.

Dame Mary Donaldson

SEA VIEW

Before snorkelling or scuba-diving – or any sub-aqua sport – the quickest and easiest way to stop your mask from fogging up is to rub spit over the inside of the visor.

Simon Hunter
Rugby player

SPEEDWALKING

Instead of jogging try speedwalking – it's less strain on the joints and has the same cardiac and aerobic benefit. Walk normally (not like a professional marathon walker) but keep up a brisk, steady pace and include a few hills. Swing your arms, put your whole body into it. Try three miles, three or four times a week; 55 minutes is reasonable, 50 good and 45 excellent. As well as being good for your heart, arteries and waistline, the rush of oxygen into the bloodstream leaves your mind dazzlingly clear and gives you a feeling of well-being.

Elizabeth Adler
Novelist

CHILDREN

Children are a great comfort in your old age – and they help you to reach it faster too.

LIONEL M. KAUFMAN

BURPING BABY

I always used to pat my babies on the back to bring up their wind, and they were promptly sick down the back of my neck. On a recent trip to Canada I watched a friend pumping her baby's arm up and down while it sat quietly on her knee. The pumping soon induced a happy burp without mishap.

Mrs Ben Yeats-Brown

TALC SOLUTION

Take a tin of talc along with the picnic for a day at the beach. Sprinkled on sandy skin, the talc absorbs moisture and the sand just brushes away.

Mary Tolley

BATH-TIME TREAT

If you have small children to stay for the night (or more), it is a good idea to put them in a bath, put the bath-rack between them, and serve supper for them on it. Drumsticks of chicken are very popular, or anything that can be eaten with the fingers. This means that your dining-room table, chairs and floor remain perfectly clean, and the children can be sponged down after the feast.

Elizabeth Jane Howard
Novelist

LABEL THE KIDS

Happy days out can be ruined by losing a favourite toy – or a child! For peace of mind tie a small label on both before setting out.

Margaret Bennett
Schoolteacher

CAN'T-BE-LOST MITTENS

To stop toddlers' mittens scattering like autumn leaves, attach one to each end of a long piece of elastic and thread it through their coat sleeves. Then, even if they pull off the mittens, they can't lose them.

Mrs Anne Morrison
Foster-mother

WELLIE WATCH

When you send little ones to school, mark their wellingtons clearly, sticking a label on the inside leg of each boot, so that they are easy to identify and the child can see at a glance which way round to put them on.

Lynne Mackaness
Primary schoolteacher

LEARNING TO WRITE LETTERS

Don't just teach your children to write thank-you letters. When the right opportunity arises give them the experience of writing the more difficult kind, like letters of condolence. Children have an instinctive understanding of loss, so learning to express sympathy when they're young is a big help in later years.

Rosemary Chester
Former headmistress

REPOSITIONED

Children love to festoon their walls with posters, but what a mess when they come down – even Blu-Tack eventually leaves a mark. I use toothpaste: when it hardens it makes a perfect glue, and will wash off afterwards.

Cathy Pennock
Stockbroker

NOT SO DARK

When my children were small they hated the dark, and as soon as I had turned out the light they would wail to have it on again. That's when we would do the 'magic'. This involved shutting our eyes tightly while we counted to twenty. When we opened them again the room seemed much lighter – as if by magic. We still do it when we walk out into a dark night.

The Lady Wardington

KEEPING THE RECORD STRAIGHT

When my daughter, now a mother herself, asked me if she had ever had mumps, I couldn't remember. I had religiously kept a record of all her baby illnesses, but had given it up when she reached her teens. One forgets, I think, that some childish illnesses strike later. Also, that grandchildren will eventually become part of the cycle and health records should be kept well into adulthood so that you can always refer back to them.

Mrs Howard Bannister

ANIMALS

*Animals are such agreeable friends – they ask no
questions, they pass no criticisms.*

GEORGE ELIOT

NEW ARRIVALS

If your dog has given birth to a litter, cut a strip of
cloth for each puppy and place these in the bed
with the mother. When the puppies go to their
new homes, send the strip along with them. It will
comfort the puppy when it misses its mother and
keep it from crying.

Lavinia, Duchess of Norfolk

THE BEST PAPER

Research carried out over a series of litters has
proved to me that the best paper for lining a puppy
run is the *Financial Times*.

Mrs John Pope

HAPPY PUPPY

To comfort a young puppy, put a ticking clock in
its basket, along with a hot-water bottle, both
wrapped in a blanket.

Mrs Lionel Green

GLUE CURE

Superglue put on a dog's cut will seal the edges until you can reach a vet. It can also be used for human cuts and was, I'm told, developed for such a use in Vietnam during the war there.

Joyce Stranger
Dog breeder

KEEP OFF THE GRASS

It is seriously believed in Australia and New Zealand that a plastic bottle sitting in the middle of the lawn will stop dogs fouling the grass. It is a strange sight to see lawn after Ramsey Street lawn sporting a plastic bottle. It seems unlikely that it works but 100,000 Australians can't be wrong!

John Petrie
Winegrower

DRY DOG

I always dry my golden retriever with a wash-leather. Its coat comes up so silky and it is the work of a moment to wring out the leather ready for the next rub.

Blind old lady in the park

TRAPPY

To stop a dog or cat sleeping on a chair or sofa, set a mousetrap and leave it on the seat. (Be sure to remove it before guests arrive.)

Ann Bellah Copeland

JUST REWARDS

If you have an environment that will suit a cat – get one. Get a kitten, or better still, two. Siblings are best. Smother them with affection. They will return that affection in a mysterious way. Your anxieties will diminish, you will sleep sounder and you will live longer. Scientists have confirmed this so I could be wrong.

Johnny Morris
Writer and broadcaster

GENTLY DOES IT

If you want your cat to wear an identity tag and bell but are afraid a conventional collar may catch on things, make one out of Velcro. Cut the collar lengthways from the soft side and fasten it with a short strip from the rough side. Your cat may occasionally come home without his collar but at least he won't be throttled!

Robert Edwards
Former Fleet Street editor

HOT CATS

For a cat who is suffering from the heat, wrap an old towel round a frozen cool-pack and stroke her gently and slowly with it. She may look a bit surprised at first, but will soon purr with pleasure.

Mary Hodge
Royal College of Physicians

SCRATCHING POST

Stop cats from clawing the curtains by making them a scratching post from an old piece of carpet nailed to a log. Every time they attack your favourite fabric, pick them up firmly and deposit them by the post. A scattering of catnip helps to attract their attention and keep them there.

Felix Kelly
Artist

WHITER THAN WHITE

A Victorian wheeze for a grey horse. If you put coal in a bucket of water and sponge him down with it, his coat will look much whiter.

Mrs Ian Maitland-Hume

ADVANCE AND RETREAT

If a horse or pony turned out in a field refuses to be caught, try the 'advance and retreat' method perfected by the great Californian horseman, Monty Roberts. Instead of pursuing the horse, chase it away from you. Then wander near, but don't look it in the eye. Try stroking its neck, but if it refuses, chase it away. Keep this up, and eventually the animal will follow you. This is called 'join up'. It sounds amazing, but it really does work – you'll be able to catch your horse easily.

Michael Clayton
Editor, Horse and Hound

KNEES UP

Horses sometimes bang their knees on the stable door, making a maddening noise and damaging their joints. A branch of monkey-puzzle tree fastened to the place of contact is much kinder than barbed wire.

The Hon. Christopher Brooke

POWDERING THE PILLS

Pills so often need to be crushed, especially if they have to be mixed into an animal's food. I always squash them between two teaspoons: they become powder in moments.

The Hon. Helen Pease

IN SICKNESS AND IN HEALTH

*If you resolve to give up smoking, drinking and loving,
you don't actually live longer; it just seems longer.*

CLEMENT FREUD

ON THE MEND

The Harley Street doctor who told me this said I'd put him out of business if I passed it on! The best remedy for cuts is Friars' Balsam, applied when the bleeding's stopped and followed after three days by Vaseline. Cuts heal without a mark, including nicks when you're shaving.

Terry Spinks
Former boxing champion

WHAT A RELIEF!

Agonizing indigestion can be relieved by pumping one's arms up and down. Raise them high above your head and bring them down to your sides several times, fairly vigorously.

Mrs Ben Yeats-Brown

QUITE BALMY

Whenever I get indigestion I slice a few slivers off a ginger bulb and pour boiling water on it. Sipping the infusion brings almost instant relief.

John Standing
Actor

CORK THE CRAMP

Everyone who suffers from cramp has a pet cure. Mine is a cork in the bed.

Andrew Duff-Gordon
Art dealer

HEEL-SAVERS

Lying in bed on your back for any length of time can be surprisingly hard on the heels. Fill a pair of rubber gloves – surgical ones are best – with water and tie a knot at each wrist. You than have two soft, non-slip cushions for your heels.

Sister Georgina Murrell
Princess Grace Hospital

SIT-UPS

Any back sufferer knows that one of the worst moments is trying to get out of bed. There comes a time when you have to brace your back to sit up, and the pain is horrendous. The solution is to tie a sheet to the end of your bed on which you can gently haul yourself up. If you do this slowly, taking the strain with your arms, you can evade the back pain.

Elizabeth Jane Howard
Novelist

... As a paraplegic, I use an aid that consists quite simply of about nine feet of cord tied round one of the legs at the feet of the bed, with a few plain knots in it to provide an easy grip. One simply hauls oneself up into a sitting position. The cord is easy to pack when one travels.

The Duke of Buccleuch

HAY FEVER

To relieve hay fever, put a few drops of Friars' Balsam into a bowl of hot water, cover your head with a towel and inhale the steam.

Barry Pluke
Physiotherapist

FEELING FINE

To prevent all forms of pregnancy sickness, take Vitamin B6.

Dame Barbara Cartland
Novelist

HELP FOR HICCUPS

My cure for hiccups is to sip a little vinegar and water – they go.

Beryl Reid
Actress

... To stop hiccups, block your nose and ears with your fingers and sip water at the same time. Someone else has to hold the glass, of course, so if it doesn't stop the hiccups at least everyone has a good laugh.

Told to Bridget Fox-Andrews
by Sir Malcolm Sargent

EASING THE ACHES

One tablespoonful of cider vinegar and a teaspoonful of honey in hot water taken every morning will help osteoarthritis.

Mrs Walter Marais

QUEASY?

If you suffer from queasiness on sea, land or in the air, wear a Sea-Band (made by Sea-Band, Church Walk, Hinckley, Leics) on each wrist. The band has a button which fits over a pressure point three fingers' width from the wrist crease. It's magical and there are no after-effects. P.S. I should add that they're no help backing winners.

Peter O'Sullevan
Racing commentator

COMING DOWN TO EARTH

If you've had a cold or blocked sinuses, coming down in an aeroplane can be torture. A Sudafed tablet before the flight and a short blast with a nasal spray such as Otravine half an hour before the descent can be wonderfully beneficial.

Dr John Tasker
General practitioner

BODY SHIFT

Walking up and down the stairs *backwards* once a day is a good exercise for 're-educating' little-used muscles, and particularly helpful for anyone recuperating from minor hip and leg injuries.

Barry Pluke
Physiotherapist

LOSING WEIGHT

If you want to lose weight and can't be bothered with complicated diets, help is at hand! There are only three rules to my diet, but if you keep strictly to them you can lose two pounds in a week.

Rule one: Eat no bread, pasta, rice or potatoes.

Rule two: Eat only food that traditionally requires the use of cutlery. Do not touch food of any kind with your hands.

Rule three: Eat only three times a day.

Gyles Brandreth
TV personality

DECEIVING THE EYE

The most painless way to cut down the amount you eat is to serve it on smaller plates. That way you get something of everything but less of it.

Rose Pelly
Student officer's secretary, Inner Temple

SPLASH!

Always splash your tits with cold water when you get out of the bath. I've been doing it since I was fourteen and lots of other parts of me have dropped, but they don't seem to have.

Jilly Cooper
Writer

SLEEP EASY

Saying night prayers can get one to sleep faster than any pill.

Father Alastair Russell
Roman Catholic priest

INSOMNIA

The secret of getting to sleep is to concentrate on something impersonal – hence the custom of counting sheep. My cure for insomnia is to go through the alphabet, matching each letter to a city – A for Aberdeen etc. Sometimes I think of a British city and then a foreign one. I've usually dropped off long before I get to Z.

Dr Alexander Burnfield
Psychiatrist

LOOKING GOOD

Presently Ethel came back in her best hat and a lovly velvit coat of royal blue. Do I look nice in my get up she asked.

Mr Salteena survayed her. You look rather rash my dear your colors dont quite match your face.

The Young Visiters
DAISY ASHFORD

THE RIGHT COLOUR

A smashing outfit in the wrong colours (for you) is a bad investment. When choosing clothes, hold the colour near your face and be brutally honest. Colours that compliment your own natural colouring can work more magic for your looks than a week at a health farm or any cosmetic wizardry.

Mary Spillane
Image consultant

TRYING IT OUT

Before buying a straight skirt, especially if it's short, find a chair and practice sitting down and getting up. Many's the time I've had to stand at a party because I knew that, once I sat, it would rise to embarrassing heights – sofas are particularly lethal.

Mercia Watkins
PR Director

PRACTICE SESSIONS

Don't take new clothes home and then forget about them. Try them on, and get used to them. This is especially true of hats.

David Shilling
Hat designer

CREATING AN IMPRESSION

It's far easier to make an inexpensive dress look expensive with good accessories than the other way round.

Mrs Bryan Jenks

UP-DATE

Last year's dress worn with this year's accessories always works. This year's dress with last year's accessories never works.

Roland Klein
Fashion designer

GOODBYE, OLD FRIEND

It's perfectly true what the fashion experts say – that if you haven't worn certain clothes in your wardrobe for over a year, the chances are you're never going to wear them. So be ruthless: take them to a dress agency if you must, or give them to charity.

Judith Hall
Editor, Woman's Weekly

HEMLINES

If you have pressed a hem until it looks like a knife edge, when you want to let it down you will not be able to without it showing. So just leave the hem gently rolled and never press along the edge or within a quarter of an inch of it.

The Rt. Hon. Mrs Margaret Thatcher
MP

ON THE SLIDE

I always snip out the shoulder-pads stitched inside lightweight tops, sweaters and dresses. The shoulder line looks much more natural if the pads are worn snug to the body rather then moving with the fabric of the top. Shoulder pads *can* be tucked under bra straps, but ideally they should be attached with short loops fastened with press studs. No safety pins, please!

Liz Smith
Fashion editor, The Times

DOUBLE TIGHTS

By the strange looks I get when visitors notice my one-legged tights hanging on the washing line, I deduce that most women do not cut off the laddered leg of a damaged pair of tights and team it up with another one-legged pair of the same colour.

Mrs Guy Woolfenden

CUPBOARD LOVE

Hang clothes you're not likely to be wearing for a while inside out – it stops them getting dusty. And if your cupboard is too short to accommodate a full-length dress, turn it inside out, sew loops to the waistband, and hang it up as you would an ordinary skirt. This also take the weight off the top of the dress and helps to hold the shape of silk jersey and other stretchy fabrics.

Liz Smith
Fashion editor, The Times

A QUESTION OF COMFORT

All shoes should be immediately comfortable. The idea that they will become increasingly more so is an illusion.

Sir Edward Rayne
Shoemaker

FEELING THE PINCH?

If your new leather shoes feel a bit tight, pour a small amount of boiling water into each shoe in turn. Leave them for no more than six seconds, pour the water away, and put on the shoes. The leather will have softened sufficiently for your feet to stretch them so that you no longer feel the pinch.

Colin McDowell
Fashion writer

BOTTLED IDEAS

Don't buy expensive boot trees – use empty bottles (I use Perrier but you should experiment to find the right shape and size). They keep boots standing upright neatly, and bottles are easy to take out and put back. Another idea from the wine cellar is to put a wire wine-rack in the bottom of your coat cupboard. It keeps brogues, or outdoor shoes of any kind, separately and neatly – and holds a lot.

Dinah Sheridan
Actress

FLAMING JUNE

The 'going' at Ascot, Henley, garden parties and marquee weddings can be soft, damp and ruinous to heels, especially if they are fabric-covered. Solve the problem by wrapping the heels in clear sticky tape. This keeps out the damp, stops staining, is invisible, and peels off easily afterwards.

Colin McDowell
Fashion writer

PEARLS OF WISDOM

Hairspray and scent will ruin your pearls. Always spray *before* you put them on.

Kiki MacDonough
Jewellery designer

BOW-TIED

Slip on several long ropes of pearls and tie them together close to the neck with a good fat black velvet bow, or any colour ribbon as long as it's not too skimpy. Where you tie the bow – beneath the chin, to one side, at the nape of the neck – is up to you, your dress and the occasion.

Ken Lane
Jewellery designer

SEEN AT A GLANCE

I hang my necklaces and belts on rows of brass hooks inside the door of my clothes cupboard. They are much easier to see and don't get all tangled up – more decorative too.

Carrie McArdle
Journalist

RINGS OF CONFIDENCE

When washing your hands away from home, never put your rings on the side of the basin: keep them in your mouth. This way there is no chance of losing them.

Mrs Ralph Medley

KEEPING MAKE-UP TIDY

I put a knife-box made of basketwork in my make-up drawer to divide lipsticks from eye make-up, foundation, etc. This can easily be kept on a dressing-table as it looks nice and is simple to clean.

The Lady Hereford

PAINTBOX COLOURS

Few models or make-up artists bother to carry a battery of lipstick cases round with them. What they do is buy an ordinary paintbox, dig out the little squares, and pour in their own colours. This may sound a tricky operation, but it isn't. All it involves is putting a small amount of lipstick (unfinished ends are ideal) into the bowl of a teaspoon and holding it briefly over a flame. The lipstick softens in seconds and firms up just as quickly with a smooth, glossy shine.

Emma Kotch
Make-up instructor

THE DAMP SPONGE TECHNIQUE

It's important, when applying foundation with a damp sponge, that the sponge should be neither too damp nor too dry. To get exactly the right consistency, hold it in cold water, and squeeze. Then place it in a tissue, and squeeze again.

Stephen Glass
Make-up analyst

FADE OUT

To hide bluish shadows under the eyes, mix a little orange corrective cream (Greasepaint make one) with concealer and stroke it on with a brush before applying foundation. By the same token, green corrective cream under foundation tones down highly coloured cheeks.

Fliff Lidsey
Co-owner of casting agency

NO MISTAKES

For quick correction of mistakes when applying make-up, dip one end of a cotton bud in non-oily eye make-up remover and squeeze it out, so that you have one damp and one dry end to tackle disasters.

Joan Price
Joan Price's Face Place

LASHES OF LASHES

As eyeshadow tends to drop on to your lashes, remember to mascara them above as well as below. This also makes them look thicker.

Vanessa Neal
Beautician

BIG EYES

To make your eyes look larger, use a white eye pencil to draw a line on the inside rim, just above the lower lashes.

The Lady May

EASY EYE MAKE-UP REMOVER

Castor oil is a perfect eye make-up remover. Make a cotton-wool pad by dipping a ball of cotton wool into water and squeezing it out. Put a few drops of castor oil on to the pad and apply it to your eye make-up.

Lady Moore

SIMPLY SMOOTH

To control unruly eyebrows, put a small amount of hairspray or gel on to an eyebrow brush and stroke them into shape.

Julie Hart
Model

BLENDING IN THE BLUSHER

The general rule for knowing where to place blusher is to find the point where a line drawn down from the edge of your eyebrow would meet a line drawn across from the corner of your nostril. This is a good starting point from which to blend the blusher either upwards or outwards, depending on whether you want to add length or breadth to your face.

Stephen Glass
Make-up analyst

A SMOOTHER TAN

Use body lotion before applying 'fake-tan' to give

a smoother texture – and then put it on with a damp sponge. And to ensure an even natural tan, use a body scrub for a couple of weeks before your holiday.

Vanessa Neal
Beautician

STAYING POWER

To give lipstick more staying power, apply it in the normal way, and blot it with a tissue. Then – and this is the trick – give it a light dusting of powder before adding the second coat.

Sarah Hedley
Model

CUCUMBER FRESH

A few slices of cucumber dabbed on to your face before you put on your make-up will freshen and tone your skin without making it too dry.

Lady Moore

AVOCADO CREAM

After peeling an avocado, rub the inside of the skin on to your hands and elbows. It absorbs easily and is the most wonderful skin cream.

Gina Fratini
Fashion designer

CLEAN TEETH

To keep teeth shiny and bright, brush them occasionally with salt.

Mrs Nigel Talbot-Rice

COLD STORAGE

Nail varnish doesn't go thick and blobby if you keep it in the fridge.

Beryl Downing
Journalist

BEAUTY GARDENING

Before gardening (or doing any really dirty job) scrape your fingernails along a bar of softened soap and paste it around the quicks too. As you scrub with a nail brush when you wash your hands afterwards, it will give you cleaner nails than you've had for days, and avoids ingrained dirt.

Sue Lawley
TV presenter

STRONG NAILS

A cube of jelly, dissolved in hot water, taken each morning with breakfast, will ensure thick, glossy hair and strong nails.

Anouska Hempel
Fashion designer

NATURAL RINSES

Pour a mixture of vinegar and water – one part vinegar to three of water – over dark hair to make it shiny. If the water is hard and your hair is fair, use diluted lemon juice. Rinse very well with cold water after either application.

Geneura Niccolini

A REAL TONIC

Henna wax mixed with a little wheatgerm oil makes a natural hair tonic. Comb it into the ends of your hair. Wrap your head in cling-film and a hot towel so that it really penetrates, and after ten minutes shampoo in the usual way.

Tracy Hilston
Hair stylist

DRIED OUT

The best treatment I know for dry or damaged hair is a fifty-fifty mixture of mayonnaise and Mazola oil. Wet your hair, apply mixture and wrap in plastic so that the whole head gets really warm. (Cling-film is ideal as it reaches body temperature quickly.) Leave the mixture on for half an hour before shampooing. But as oil and water don't mix, be sure to apply the shampoo *first*, working it well in, and add the water *second*.

Douglas von Katzer
The Bute Street Salon

UNCONDITIONED

So many people apply conditioner in quite the wrong way. It does not need to go on your scalp at all. Rub it well into the ends of your hair and keep it clear of the roots, which it will clog if you are not careful.

Laurence Anthony
Hair stylist

SOAP IT SMOOTH

If you are without hairspray, apply moist soap – in the theatre we always used it during the war. Just leave wet soap on your hands after washing and apply it to the offending areas of loose or straggly hair.

Dame Beryl Grey
Prima ballerina

THE BEAUTY OF BRAIDS

If your hair is long enough to plait, weave in a coloured ribbon. It's easy to do. Instead of dividing the hair into three sections, you divide it into two and use the ribbon as the third. If your hair is short, invest in a false plait, braiding it with ribbon in the same way, to pin on in the evenings.

Douglas von Katzer
The Bute Street Salon

HATS ON

The foolproof way to keep your hat on in a high wind is to wind a strand of hair round two small rollers – one to the front, one at the back – push them up out of sight and stick your hatpins firmly into them through the brim.

The Lady Porchester

DRINKING

*I'm only a beer tee-totaller, not a champagne
tee-totaller.*

GEORGE BERNARD SHAW

VERY MORE-ISH

The most more-ish drink I know is iced tea, and
this is my favourite recipe. Choose Ceylon tea,
which does not cloud, and make it slightly
stronger than usual – an extra teaspoonful will do.
Then strain the tea into a jug in which you've put
a little sugar and some ice cubes. When you are
ready to serve the tea, but not before, garnish it
with lemon or cucumber slices or bruised mint
leaves.

Sam Twining

NICE AND EASY

The most delicious iced coffee is easily made with two tablespoons of Camp coffee added to a pint of milk with lots of ice.

Kevin Thorpe
Conservative agent

COFFEE CHOCOLATE

Fresh coffee, once opened, soon loses its aroma. To restore it, add a cube of plain chocolate to the pot just before serving. A teaspoon of cocoa powder would do, but chocolate is best.

Roland Klein
Fashion designer

WHAT THE EYE DOESN'T SEE

Stick a coffee bean under a blazing grill while serving your guests Nescafé – the aroma deceives them into thinking it's superb freshly ground Blue Mountain or something.

Alice Thomas Ellis
Author

QUICK WARM-UP

Very hot Bovril with a good shot of sherry in it is wonderfully warming when you have that chilled-to-the-marrow feeling.

Esme Boughey
Northants organizer, National Gardens Scheme

A CLEAR CONSCIENCE

To get over the guilt of drinking, take your brandy in milk. This way, it becomes medicinal.

Catherine Cookson
Novelist

POIRE WILLIAM

A wonder, like a ship in a bottle, is a liqueur with a beautiful big pear floating in the bottle. If you have a pear tree you can make this yourself. Find a nice young pear in the early summer and insert it, still on the tree, into a bottle. Tie the bottle firmly to the tree and wait for the pear to ripen on the branch. When the pear is ready, cut it off and fill the bottle with your favourite spirit. Seal the bottle well and wait for as long as you can before drinking.

Rex Johnston-Smith
Retired diplomat

COOK'S NIPS

This is a great solace to the cook, and very much enjoyed by guests who may wander into the kitchen. Take one large glass jar with a tightly fitting lid, place eight prunes in the bottom and cover them with brandy. As available, add bottle ends of any spirits or liqueurs, remembering at all times that every little counts. Stir the potion occasionally as it matures and darkens. Sampling by the cook should occur regularly once the jar is half full. Keep it in a secure place!

Diana Chesney

THE RIGHT WAY ROUND

When mixing spirits with a soft drink, e.g. whisky and soda or gin and tonic, most people put the spirit in the glass first. Put them in the other way round and you will get a much better mix, as you are drinking the soft drink through the spirit.

The Hon. Peter Ward
Katharine House Hospice Appeal, Chairman

SERIOUSLY COLD

Always keep a bottle of gin and plenty of tonic in the fridge. The coldness of the gin and tonic will ensure that the ice does not melt too quickly.

David Astor

ICED VODKA

A stylish way to serve really cold vodka is to cut the top off a two-litre Coca-Cola bottle, place the full vodka bottle inside it and fill up the surrounding space with cold water, leaving the neck well out. Place it in the freezer long enough for the water to freeze solid (the vodka won't) and release from the plastic bottle by running it briefly under the cold tap. You then have a perfect ice collar round the whole bottle. Stand the vodka bottle on something suitable to catch any drips from the melting ice.

Michael Mander

LEMON ICES

When slicing a lemon for use in a gin and tonic, cut the remaining part into small pieces and place them with water in the ice-cube tray. Freeze and use when next serving this drink.

Mrs John Major

THE LAST DROP

Five minutes or so after emptying a bottle of gin, whisky or whatever, tip the bottle into the glass again and a small but pleasing reward will have appeared. This is known as an Uncle Bertie, after the darling man who taught it to us. You can also apply Uncle Bertie to underarm roll-on at the end of its life – left upside down it provides at least another week of charmpits.

Derek Collins
Apartment agent

A GREAT IMPROVEMENT

Cheap champagne can be much improved by pouring it into a jug before serving.

The Hon. William Pease
Ear, nose and throat surgeon

WASTE NOT

How to keep the fizz in your half-empty bottle of champagne if you haven't got a stopper: hang a teaspoon in the neck, handle down, and replace the bottle in the fridge. Don't ask why it works but it does – for up to two days.

Diana Rigg
Actress

ONE QUICK TWIST

When opening a bottle of champagne, always use a pair of nutcrackers. With a quick twist the cork is out.

John Julius Norwich
Writer and broadcaster

CORK IT

If the cork from a half-empty bottle of wine refuses to go back in, pour boiling water over the cork until it's soft – then push.

Mrs Ivo Reid

THE HOT WATER WAY

When the cork just won't budge in the wine bottle, turn it horizontal and play a hot tap over the neck, rotating it as you do so, for sixty seconds. The glass will expand very slightly and lose its vice-like grip on the cork so that it comes out with gratifying ease. Don't worry about the wine. Being hot under the collar for such a brief time will not, in my experience, harm even the most noble white Burgundy. If, however, you are still worried about the top of the bottle being affected, drink the first glass yourself. I always do.

Godfrey Smith
Journalist and writer

EMERGENCY MEASURES

Desperate situations call for desperate measures. At sun-downer time on safari in Zimbabwe I found myself with an unopened bottle of wine and no corkscrew. The guide grasped the bottle very firmly with both hands and instructed me to thwack its bottom with my rubber-soled shoe. Slowly but surely the cork inched its way out of the neck. Perhaps this is not to be recommended for vintage claret or champagne, but it's effective!

Alexander Pease
Solicitor

A KNOTTY PROBLEM

When the cork breaks just as you are pulling it out of a wine bottle, all is not lost if you perform this simple operation. Push the cork right into the bottle, and tie a knot in a piece of string. Drop the string, knot end first, into the wine so that the knot is below the cork and tilt the bottle so that the cork comes into the neck. Pull on the string and the knot will bring the cork out. It sounds complicated but it is in fact quite easy.

The Earl of Westmorland

INSTANT AERATION

When there isn't time to allow your treasured claret to breathe for the hour or so it needs to develop, the following approach will achieve the same effect in minutes. Arm yourself with two jugs and decant the bottle carefully into one; then pour the wine into the other from a height. Repeat the process a couple of times – a 'big' wine needs more repeats, but don't overdo it.

Derek Jones
Wine merchant

COOLING DOWN

White wines are happiest when they are gently chilled in the fridge, but if you get caught out by an unexpected guest, the swiftest way of chilling white wine is to submerge the bottle in an ice-bucket filled with ice and water. Avoid putting the bottle in the deep-freeze, but if you *must*, ten minutes is all that is required.

Jane MacQuitty
Wine correspondent, The Times

BEAMING IN

A bright light from beneath greatly assists decanting. Try a Durabeam torch. Its swivel head and concentrated beam are much more effective than a candle.

Duncan McEuan
Christie's wine department

KNOCK ON GLASS

When the stopper of a glass decanter is firmly stuck, tap it gently with another glass stopper. It works every time.

Michael Brand
Antiquarian bookseller

… When the stopper of my decanter gets stuck I run hot water on its neck, taking care to keep the stopper cool. After a moment or two it comes out.

Nicholas Courtney
Writer

LACQUER THE LABELS

If, like me, you have a damp cellar, spray the labels of all your wine bottles with hair lacquer before putting them in the racks. This will remove from your wife any excuse, a year or two down the line, for giving the Leoville Barton '82 to the local bazaar on the grounds that she had no means of knowing that it was not Rioja.

Max Hastings
Editor, The Daily Telegraph

FOOD

STORING IT

THE AROMA OF SUMMER

If you want the fresh taste of your summer herbs to last through the winter, try stuffing them into a bottle until you can get no more in, and then fill the bottle up with olive oil and stand it in the sun. After a day or two pour off the oil (if it's basil you put in) or a week or two (if it's tarragon), let the oil separate from the juice and pour it off. A drop or two of the oil in salad dressing or in mayonnaise, or on spaghetti, brings back all the aroma of summer.

Germaine Greer
Author and lecturer

MAKING THE MOST OF HERBS

For culinary or medical herbs and spices to yield fully their flavour and substance, they should be kept away from light and in cool, dry conditions – not in the kitchen over the cooker.

R. A. Hill
British Herbal Medicine Association

BOTTLE ENDS

To prevent a small amount of wine left in a bottle from going off, pour in half a teaspoonful of olive oil. The wine will then keep for some weeks – not for drinking, of course, but for cooking.

Dorothy Tutin
Actress

STORING GARLIC

Cloves of peeled garlic will keep for months if you cover them with olive oil and store them in a screw-topped jar, topping up with more oil as you use them. The oil takes on the flavour of the garlic and makes delicious salad dressings. (Olives left over from a half-used tin can be stored in the same way, but be sure to rinse them first.)

Katie Stewart
Cookery writer

SAVING TOMATO PASTE

If you have only half used a tube or pot of tomato paste, put the rest into an ice-cube tray and freeze it ready for next time.

Mrs Ivo Reid

CRUMBLED PARSLEY

Keep bunches of parsley in the freezer. When you need chopped parsley just crumble it while it is still frozen. In fact this works with all herbs. Use the stalks for the stock pot.

Mrs Iain Campbell-Blair

IN MINT CONDITION

When mint is new and young, cut about three inches off the top of each stalk, lay the sprigs on a plate and put it in the freezer. When the mint is frozen, place it carefully in a plastic box. In the depths of winter it's lovely to be able to decorate melon or prawn cocktails with a sprig of fresh mint – but don't take it out of the freezer until immediately prior to serving.

Jan Leeming
TV presenter

… In the summer I chop mint with lots of sugar and freeze it in a large carton. Sugar stops the mint from freezing solid and keeps its colour fresh. When I want to make mint sauce I spoon out the amount I need and mix it with vinegar.

Michael Graham
Hotelier

FULL OF BEANS

I adore freshly ground coffee and always buy my beans in seven-pound bags – it's so much cheaper that way. I keep the beans in the freezer, grind as many as I need while they're still frozen, and make the coffee straight away.

Christopher Biggins
Actor

NUTS!

Recently someone advised me that freezing pistachio nuts was a wonderful way to keep them fresh and make them last longer. So when I travel abroad and find them at a more reasonable price I bring back a bag, or ask a friend to, and pop them in the freezer. You can then take out as many as you want for a particular occasion; they need only a few minutes out of the freezer before they are wonderfully crisp and fresh.

Deborah Owen
Literary agent

USE YOUR LOAF

My bachelor stand-by was always to keep a loaf of *sliced* thick white bread in the freezer, as you can use it to make toast without defrosting. Just break off a couple of slices and put them straight in the toaster.

Julian Fellowes
Actor

PLENTY OF PUFF

Pitta bread freezes well and defrosts quickly. It does tend to harden up when you toast it, though, so do what the restaurateurs do: run it quickly under hot water before putting it on the grill and it will puff up beautifully.

Ossie Osai
Beauty photographer

FROZEN BANANAS

You *can* freeze bananas. Their skins go black but the insides are quite all right.

Kate Thompson
Norland nanny

KEEPING EGGWHITES

Did you know that you can freeze left-over eggwhites? They will keep for up to a year in the freezer and can be defrosted and whisked up when needed.

Nancy, the Lady Blakenham

MOIST AND FRESH

To keep fruit cake moist, store it in a tin with an eating apple. To keep watercress longer, put it in a bowl of water, *stalks up*.

Lady Wade

SALT SOLUTION

Add two grains of rice to the salt cellar and you'll never have damp salt again.

Margaret Raven

SOFTENING BROWN SUGAR

When soft brown sugar has gone hard – when does it not? – take the lid off the container and cover the sugar with a damp cloth overnight. It will be soft again in the morning. Or put a slice of soft white bread or an apple into the container. But if you're desperate, hack off the required amount and grate it.

Mrs John Seyfried

TIGHT STORAGE

Onions and apples keep well in tights. Drop one down to the toe and tie a knot; drop in another and keep knotting until each leg is full. Then just hang up and cut off as you need them.

Anne Abbott

BAGGY

Lettuce or parsley – or any green leaf – keeps fresh and crispy for up to three weeks if you put it in the fridge in a large polythene bag loosely tied at the top. The trick is to make sure there is lots of air trapped in the bag.

Angela Pitt
Directors' lunch cook

PEGGING THE PACKET

Keep opened cereal packets tightly closed with a couple of clothes pegs.

The Hon. Mrs Williams

PREPARING IT

UP THE SPOUT

In my haste to make a cuppa, I discovered that by placing the teapot on the spout of the electric kettle, the steam heats the teapot precisely as it should.

Terence Stamp
Actor

A GOOD SPREAD

Whenever friends see me do this they always say

'What a good idea – I never thought of that.'
When slicing and buttering bread it is best to
butter the loaf and *then* slice it. I have a feeling it
is a working-class habit so your surprise may
depend on where you were brought up.

Eileen Atkins
Actress

EGGOCENTRIC

I am slightly fussy about my boiled eggs. I like the
white to be softly firm and the yoke to be yellow
and creamy, so I do them in this rather eccentric
way. Bring the water to the boil in a small
saucepan. Switch off the gas. Put the egg in. Cover
the pan with a saucer or a plate and leave the egg
for ten minutes in the slowly cooling water. This
way I achieve my perfect morning boiled egg.

Ronnie Corbett
Comedian

PUT TO THE TEST

To test whether an egg is fresh, place it in a bowl of
water. If the egg floats it is bad. To test whether an
egg is raw or hard-boiled, spin it. If it whirls like a
top it is hard-boiled; if it just wobbles it is raw.

Nigel Talbot-Rice
Headmaster of Summerfields

GULLS' EGGS – BOILED OR RAW

Gulls' eggs are best bought raw, in which
condition they will keep for a month in the fridge.
To cook them, put them in a pan of cold water,
bring it to the boil and simmer for seven minutes.
Cool immediately.

The Hon. Mrs Pease

GLORIOUS GROUSE

Cut the neck and wings off game with a pair of scissors *before* plucking. Contrary to popular fears, it should then take no more than four or five minutes to strip. Finish off by singeing with a blowtorch, if you have no gas ring.

Max Hastings
Editor, The Daily Telegraph

TOGETHERNESS

Sausages are much easier to grill or fry if they are speared together side by side.

Dora Bryan
Actress

PERFECT MUSTARD

I find that English mustard, made to order, is infinitely superior to any bottled variety. The secret is to make it not with water, but with milk. It lasts seven times as long and does not turn brown.

Auberon Waugh
Editor, The Literary Review

A GOOD WARM-UP

If your Camembert cheese isn't ripe enough, wrapping it in ordinary newspaper speeds up the process remarkably quickly.

June Ducas
Journalist

... If the Brie you want to eat immediately is still hard and chalky, pop it in the microwave and give it several ten-second blasts on defrost.

It's a delicate operation, though, so watch carefully for the perfect texture.

Mrs Douglas Pennock

KIND TO ASPARAGUS

When tying asparagus into bundles for cooking, it's much kinder to use one-inch-wide cotton bandage rather than string. Wind it around the bundle several times so that the stalks won't slip, then tie tightly. This method works for slender young leeks, too, when you're cooking them to serve cold.

Katie Stewart
Cookery writer

TEARS AWAY

Peel onions under a running tap to keep the tears at bay and suck a marble or a pebble while chopping them.

Toni Palamountain

JUST ADD WATER

When chopping onions in the food processor, add water; then empty them into a sieve. This way you won't leave lots of bits in the bowl.

Milly Yates
Cook

EASY PEELING

To peel garlic effortlessly, place it on a firm surface and put a heavy flat object (a frying pan, the side of a cleaver, a weight from a scale) on top. Press down till the garlic crushes *slightly*. The papery skin will then fall off without any effort or fingernail prying.

Michael Barry
Presenter, The Crafty Cook

EASY EXTRACTION

A lemon will yield much more juice if you submerge it in water for an hour before squeezing. But you won't need to squeeze it at all if you cut it in half, then put it in a bowl and microwave it for a minute or two. The juice will just pour out.

Mrs John Joint

OLD WIVES' TALE

If a lettuce should become limp, place it in an empty saucepan with a lump of coal. Put the lid on, and after a few hours it will become crisp again.

Mrs Darling's nanny

SPEEDY RECOVERY

I revive wilted parsley by running it under cold water and then wringing it out really hard in the corner of a clean teacloth.

Laurie Purden
Journalist

DIPPY

Avocado dip or guacamole won't go brown while it waits for the party if you leave the avocado stone in it, and cover it with cling-film.

Robert Bruce
Architectural student

COLOUR CO-ORDINATION

Ingredients of the same colour can look much more striking than direct contrasts. Try mixing the varied greens of different salad varieties, or making fruit salads in co-ordinating colours – a red, yellow or green mixture served in a clear glass bowl looks simply stunning.

Katie Stewart
Cookery writer

RADISH ROSES

To turn a radish into a 'rose', make several cuts downwards from tip to base with a sharp knife. Put it into ice-cold water, and it will open up like a flower.

Barbara Murray
Actress

OIL ON TROUBLED WATERS

Pasta, rice, potatoes – or, indeed, anything that needs a full pan of water – will boil contentedly without boiling over if a few drops of oil are added to the pot. The oil breaks the surface tension of the water.

HKH Princess Lillian of Sweden

STEAMED UP

It's the work of a moment to cover a steamed pudding with aluminium foil and make a sling of another strip of foil with which to lift it in and out of the saucepan of boiling water. This method is much easier than faffing about with the more conventional greaseproof paper lid and string.

Bridget Mason
Village postmistress

FORKING THEM OVER

To de-stalk red or blackcurrants, run the prongs of a fork along the stem.

Rosa Merry

CRISP CRUST

To prevent the juice of fruit pies from soaking into the bottom crust, wash the crust over with beaten egg before putting in the fruit.

George Baker
Actor and cookery writer

BEST KEPT SECRET

Question: How to make a pavlova which does *not* stick to the vessel in which it was cooked?

Answer: Grease the dish or plate very well and then give a generous dusting with flour before piping your meringue mixture on to it.

The Viscountess Cobham

A PROFESSIONAL FINISH

When you're making biscuits, roll out the pastry and decorate it with stars by using the tip of an ordinary egg whisk.

Mrs A. King

EASY ROLLER

Roll out marzipan between sheets of cling-film – it saves a lot of mess. This works with pastry too.

Angela Uzielli
Ladies Open Golf Champion 1990

WEIGHING HONEY

When a recipe calls for a certain weight of honey or syrup, put the tin on the scales and spoon out the required amount. Also, since syrup is such sticky stuff, it helps to put any dry ingredients into the mixing bowl first and spoon the syrup on to them, so that it doesn't touch the bowl.

The Hon. Mrs Sarah Baring

JAMMY

Boiling jam develops a foamy scum which you have to skim off. All this skimming can be eliminated if at the last minute you whisk in a knob of butter: the scum will just disappear.

Mrs Gerhard Bülle

SPILL-PROOF

When I can't lay my hands on a funnel, I cut off the top quarter of an empty plastic bottle, up-end it and use that. It's particularly useful when you're doing something really messy, like storing frying oil to use again, or transferring olive oil from a large bottle into a smaller one, as you just chuck the funnel away afterwards.

Patric Walker
Astrologer

... The ideal funnel for pouring hot jam neatly into jars can be made by sawing the top off a two-litre plastic squash bottle. If you have one with a handle, leave that on to hold it by.

Mrs M. Howes

GETTING RID OF THE GREASE

Excess grease which has gathered on the surface of a stew pot can be removed by tossing in a few leaves of lettuce or any other vegetable. After a few minutes they will have absorbed the grease and can be removed.

HKH Princess Lillian of Sweden

FRESHER MICROWAVE

Sometimes when one opens the door of the microwave a waft of the last meal cooked in it hits you. To cure this, put a cut lemon in a bowl of water into the microwave and switch it on for a couple of minutes.

Leonie Richards

COOKING CABBAGE

Lemon juice in the cooking water stops cabbages from smelling. Or a small pan of vinegar and water simmering on the side of the stove will get rid of the smell.

The Lady Grantley

... We find that one or two bay leaves singed on the electric cooker gets rid of cooking smells – not burnt, just singed.

Alison Giraud-Saunders

... Stale bread dropped into the water or put in a strainer or sieve on top of the saucepan will absorb the odour of boiling vegetables.

HKH Princess Lillian of Sweden

FISHY FINGERS

If you have been working with onions or fish, lemon juice rubbed over your hands will remove the smell.

Mildred Nash
Parlourmaid

COOKING IT

QUICK QUICHE

A magical way of making instant quiche. Put
1 onion, 4 eggs, 125g/4oz butter, 250ml/8fl oz milk,
60g/2oz flour, ¹/₂ teaspoon baking powder, 60g/2oz
grated Cheddar cheese, parsley and anything else
going, into a good mixer. Whirl it all together, pour
the mixture into an appropriate dish, and bake at
190°C/375°F/ Gas Mark 6 for 40 minutes. Serves 4.

Patricia Ruck-Keene,
Hospital receptionist

HEAVENLY HAMBURGERS

When making hamburgers don't salt the meat
mixture but salt the pan – i.e. to cook the burgers,
heat the pan with a good handful of sea salt until the
pan and the salt are very hot. Then add the burgers.
They will have a flavoursome crust and the
minimum of greasiness.

Fay Maschler
Cookery writer

SALMON IN THE NEWS

For a different way to cook a whole salmon, wrap it in three or four sheets of thoroughly dampened newspaper and make a neat parcel. Put the parcel on a baking sheet and place it in the centre of a moderate oven. When the paper is dry on the top, turn the salmon over and continue cooking until the paper dries again – this can take up to one hour. If serving the salmon hot, peel off the paper and place the salmon on a dish. If serving it cold, allow it to cool before unwrapping it. In both cases the skin comes off with the paper.

Diana Chesney

SPOON-STUFFED CHICKEN

An excellent way of cooking a chicken to eat cold is to put as many spoons as you can – not silver or plated – into the carcase and submerge the chicken in a large pan of water with a few herbs. Bring the water slowly to the boil and simmer for five minutes. Let the chicken cool in the water until it is quite cold. Because the heat from the spoons cooks the chicken from the inside you will find it wonderfully succulent.

Peter Clark
Fashion photographer

CHICKEN TARRAGON

Of the many recipes for this dish I like this one best. You need 1 chicken, ¼ teaspoon of onion chopped very small, 1 heaped dessertspoon of dried tarragon (or twice the quantity of fresh), some brown stock or Bovril-and-water, cream, flour and salt.

Roast the chicken, carve it and put it in a dish to keep hot. Pour off the fat from the pan and make a gravy in the usual way with flour, salt, etc, but as you will need more than one sauceboatful, add extra flour, plus stock or Bovril-and-water. Throw in the tarragon, onion and cream, cook for a minute or two, and then either pour the sauce over the chicken, or hand it round separately. For a dinner party use two chickens and more of everything!

Anne Scott-James
Journalist

QUICK CHICK

If you are wondering what to do with left-over cooked chicken, chop it up and mix it with sliced avocado. Covered with mayonnaise and sprinkled with crumbled crispy bacon, this dish looks as good as it tastes. How many it will serve depends on how much chicken you had to start with.

Mrs V. M. Pilkington

THE WALL TEST

Spaghetti is cooked if, when you throw a strand against a tiled wall, it sticks!

Lara Nicholas
aged six

CRISP AND LIGHT

For roast potatoes that are light and floury inside and crisp outside: parboil the potatoes for about five minutes, drain well and put back into the saucepan. Sprinkle them with flour (enough to coat them), put the lid on and shake them vigorously, turning them upside down, banging the pan on the chopping board, the more violently the better, then add to the hot fat in the oven.

Monica Dickens
Author

INSTANT APPLE 'SAUCE'

Bake cooking apples alongside your joint of roast pork and you'll have instant apple 'sauce', ready to serve. Prepare and core the apples just as you would if you were going to bake them separately, adding a sprinkling of sugar if you like them sweet. Then run a knife tip around them to slit the skin so that, while cooking, the apples will puff upwards and hold their shape.

Katie Stewart
Cookery writer

DANDELION SNACKS

Chopped-up dandelion leaves in sandwiches or salads are extremely good for you and add a sharp, special flavour.

Ossie Osai
Beauty photographer

SALAD SOUP

Don't throw away left-over salad that's been tossed in dressing. Whisk it up in the food processor with a can of tomato juice or soup and lots of garlic, adjusting the quantity of liquid to suit the amount of salad available. Chill it well and you will have the most delicious summer soup, different every time you make it.

Lady Holland-Martin

CURDLE CURE

Mayonnaise which has curdled can be rescued by whisking in a spoonful or two of Hellmann's mayonnaise. Nervous cooks can play safe and start off the mayonnaise mixture with a little Hellmann's, which should remove all danger of it curdling.

Nicholas Courtney
Writer

LUMPY SAUCES

Don't panic if the sauce is lumpy. Strain it – what are strainers for!

Mrs Ann Kotch
Animator

TOO MUCH SALT

If you find at the last moment that a sauce is too salty, you can absorb it by putting a cube of sugar into a spoon and lowering it into the sauce for twenty seconds.

Roland Klein
Fashion designer

… If you have a disaster and oversalt a casserole or soup, add a diced potato and simmer until it is cooked – it absorbs the extra salt.

Beryl Downing
Journalist

SIMPLY TOPPING

I usually put this topping on a chicken pie instead of pastry but it is just as good on any savoury dish. Puncture a bag of crisps to let the air out, then scrunch up the crisps and sprinkle a generous layer over the pie. Bake in the normal way.

Mrs Peter Barker

CHEESE CRUMBLE

Put equal quantities of cheese and left-over crusts of bread into the food processor and crumble them all up together. Freeze in a plastic bag and use as required as a topping for fish pies, etc.

Hilary Westwater
Printer

TIME AND HEALTH SAVED

A banana or an avocado will replace a meal or, for that matter, so will any fresh whole fruit, saving time and trouble.

Sir Yehudi Menuhin
Violinist

MERINGUE ICE

This is a delicious made-in-a-moment sweet in which to use up meringues. Whip ½ pint of double cream with a little blanched orange zest and 3 tablespoons of Cointreau. When stiff, fold in 4oz of homemade meringues pieces, put in a pretty dish and freeze. Serve frozen (the Cointreau will stop it becoming too solid) with a scattering of toasted almonds.

The Lady Wardington

FINE FINISH

Eggwhites hold better and can be left standing if one tablespoon of the weighed sugar per egg is beaten in for a further minute after the eggwhites have been beaten to the required stiffness.

Try making crème brulée in small ramekins and use brown sugar for the top – it caramelizes quicker in small containers.

Mrs John Biffen

BRANDY-SNAP CUPS

Make brandy snaps in the usual way and store them flat in an airtight container. When you need them, place each one on the base of an upturned jamjar in a warm oven for five to ten minutes. The snaps will then droop to a cup shape and can be taken off when cooled.

Lady Howe

THE ANSWER'S A LEMON

Cheer up an ordinary Victoria sponge by adding grated lemon rind to the mixture. Mix the juice of the lemon with three tablespoons of granulated sugar and pour it over the cake as soon as you take it out of the oven. When the cake is cool, it will have a lemony sugary crust – much tastier that the usual jam filling.

Beryl Downing
Journalist

TEXTURED SPONGE

A tablespoonful of hot water, beaten into sponge mixture last thing, will greatly improve the texture of the cake.

Dora Saint
'Miss Read', *author*

DOING IT YOURSELF

If all else fails, read the instructions.

ANON.

SCREWING

For almost all screw tops – and screws in general – remember that right is tight and left is loose.

Paul Parris
Trainee barrister

TWIST AGAIN

When the lid of a screw-topped jar or bottle refuses to budge, wrap a rubber band round it and twist once more.

Mrs Alexander Pease

STONED

To get rid of a stain on porous stone, apply a poultice of household bleach and builder's plaster.

Simon Hunter
Rugby player

DON'T BE SLOPPY

It's easy, but a great mistake, to make mortar too rich in cement and too wet. The mix should be approximately 4 parts sand to 1 part cement, or, better still, 6 parts sand, 1 part lime, 1 part cement.

Ray Cherry
Master builder

AGEING GRACEFULLY

Might I suggest a trick for weathering new stone, whether real or reconstituted, which seems to have the desired effect, is to apply yoghurt, suitably watered down. This creates a patina and allows some type of growth to develop, which very quickly takes the new shine off the stone. The mixture can be quite light so it will not show.

The Marquess of Salisbury

… Cow dung, mixed with enough water so that it stays on the paintbrush, can be painted over certain types of stone and cement rendering. It gives a weathered effect and encourages lichen to grow.

Trevor Dean
Stonemason

AN AWKWARD SCREW

The task of introducing a small screw into a cramped location can be eased by placing a dab of grease on the tip of the screwdriver before inserting it in the head of the screw, which will then stick to the screwdriver.

The Lord Tombs
Chairman, Rolls-Royce

BRUISE-FREE

How many times have you hammered your thumb instead of the tintack or nail? Dozens of times in my case, until I learned to hold the nail in place with a hair pin.

Iain Campbell-Blair

CROSSED WIRES

There's no need to panic when rewiring a plug, if you remember that the bRown wire goes on the Right and the bLue wire goes on the Left.

Brian Henderson
Electrical engineer

SLOW SHOWER

Fill a plastic bag with vinegar and tie it over a sluggish shower-head so that the head is fully submerged. Leave it for a few hours and it will flow freely again.

Mrs Anthony Hopkins

BLOCKED DRAINS

If the drain of a basin is blocked, connect a hose from the tap to the plughole – you may need a jubilee clip – and turn the tap on full. The strong flow will clear the obstruction simply and cheaply.

The Earl Kitchener of Khartoum

… To clear a blocked sink put some soda down the plughole, and pour on plenty of boiling water.

Field Marshal The Lord Bramall

GETTING EVEN

Nothing is more irritating than a wobbly chair or table. Level it up by putting a dollop of plastic wood on to a piece of kitchen foil and pressing the unbalanced leg into it. When the plastic wood has dried firm, either lift off the foil or, if it won't peel, cut to shape.

The Lord Wardington

PUTTY IN YOUR HANDS

If you have some putty left over after a DIY job, put it in a plastic bag, make this airtight with a rubber band and put it in your deep freeze. When you want to use it again, take the putty out and knead it. It will be soft enough, and as new, within a few minutes.

Captain Ralph Medley

SMOOTHING OVER THE CRACKS

When filling cracks and crevices, people tend to ram in far too much filler and then have to sandpaper if off, leaving dust on the paintwork. It is much quicker and easier to work in just enough filler, and immediately 'wash' over it with a paintbrush dipped in water. The water softens the filler so that it can be smoothed over the surface and moulded into any awkward-to-get-at places.

Glenn Martins
Professional decorator

FOILED!

A loaded paintbrush will stay supple for quite a while – certainly long enough for an essential shopping trip or a leisurely coffee break – if you wrap the bristles in kitchen foil.

Wendy Gardner
Schoolteacher

NEAT BRUSHWORK

To avoid overloading your paintbrush, tie a piece of wire across the top of the paint pot and wipe your brush on this every time you pull it out. It makes a good brush rest, too.

Andrew Wilkins
Painter and decorator

SKIRTING TROUBLE

Before you re-paint skirting-boards or any area that touches close-carpeting, edge the carpet with wide brown-paper adhesive tape. It will catch the drips and is easy to pull off when the paint is dry.

Donald Derrick
Dental surgeon

A PERFECT MATCH

Wall-paint, once applied, is seldom exactly the same shade as the colour chart. To get an accurate sample for colour-matching accessories, daub a little of the paint on to a white postcard and take that with you when you go shopping.

Angela Pelly
Farmer's wife

SMALL IS BEAUTIFUL

When painting doors or windows, wash out an empty dog-food or baked-bean tin and fill it with paint from the large can. A small container is much easier to handle, and this way it stops the paint in the large can from drying out. When you have finished, simply throw the small tin away – it saves a lot of messy clearing up.

Oh, yes – another tip. You know the paint in a large can, once opened, invariably forms a nasty skin on top, which you then have to get rid of before using the paint again? Well, it won't if you store the paint can upside down. That way, the skin forms on the *bottom* – but for obvious reasons it's wise to make sure you've put the lid on really tight!

Donald Sinden
Actor

PATCHING UP

Resist the temptation to chuck out the remains of a tin of paint you've just finished using. Instead, pour it into a small screw-topped glass jar and keep it for painting over knocks and scratches.

Cherry Large
Doctor's wife

SOFT OPTION

Use cooking oil to get the paint off your hands after decorating. It is much kinder than paint remover and just as effective.

Lee Alfandary
School secretary

ANTIQUE GOLD

Gold picture frames that look too bright can be 'aged' by brushing them lightly with brown shoe polish.

Mrs Francis Sitwell

GUM THE FRAME

To renovate the moulding on gilt picture frames, chew some chewing gum and, when it's pliable, remould it to shape on the frame. Let it dry hard, then spray it with gilt.

Nan Stratton

GARDENING

*When your back stops aching and your hands
   begin to harden
You will find yourself a partner in the Glory of
   the Garden.*

RUDYARD KIPLING

THE GOOD EARTH

When making a compost heap, remember that you must always have three heaps or bins: one for fresh garden and kitchen material, one in the process of rotting down, and one ready for use. It takes two years for compost to decay, and if the different 'vintages' get mixed up, they are useless. A large open bin divided into three is ideal, but in a small garden three small containers will do. If plenty of damp material is used, watering, turning and activating should not be necessary.

Anne Scott-James
Journalist

... Instead of making the compost heap look even uglier by edging it with black polythene, cardboard or whatever, grow *Lonicera Nitida* (honeysuckle) around it, and trim it to the height of the heap. It makes a pretty surround and is easy to grow.

Mrs A. King

SEEDED EGGBOXES

Recycle old cardboard eggboxes by filling them with seed compost and planting a seed in each section. When they're ready to plant out you can cut them into sections and plant without disturbing the roots – the cardboard will simply break down.

Iris Scotchmer

THE GREENHOUSE EFFECT

If you are going away during a dry spell, create a mini-greenhouse over any plant you have just planted out. Place a clear plastic bag, with a central stick, over the watered plant and peg down the edges with twigs. You should return to find it flourishing.

The Rt. Hon. Kenneth Baker
MP

MINI-PROPAGATORS

I save all my instant coffee jars to use as tiny greenhouses. When I have taken a cutting I put a jar over the pot and leave it to grow happily in its own little propagator until it has properly taken root.

The Hon. Mrs Sergison-Brooke

EGGSHELL POTS

When I was small I lived with a governess called Miss Davis at the Lodge at Yapton. Miss Davis was a keen gardener, and I recall weeding and replanting primulas for tuppence an hour! In the early spring we began to save the shells from our breakfast boiled eggs, and at the appropriate time we planted a sweet pea seed in each shell, tapped the bottom lightly, and sat the shells on trays in the greenhouse. When it was time to plant the seedlings out, each shell was crushed gently and then placed carefully into the prepared hole. In this way the roots of the seedlings were undisturbed, and we had a 100 per cent success rate. Much cheaper than the modern equivalent!

Jacqueline Inchbald
Principal, the Inchbald School of Design

GROWING WILD

I sometimes allow special wild flowers to remain and develop in my garden. I have two at the moment, an enormous bush of wild marjoram which is six feet high and looks marvellous in the herbaceous border, and a clump of sheep's bit, which is twice its usual height and covered with a mass of bright blue flowers. Some wild flowers seem to turn into garden flowers, given water and the usual fertilizers.

The Countess of Longford
Author and biographer

MORE OF WHAT YOU'VE GOT

Always remember how many things in the garden you can easily propagate for yourself. Here are some ideas.

Lavender eventually becomes old and woody. To renew it, take cuttings in the first or second week of August. Line these out in a cold frame, and by the following spring they will have wonderful roots.

Hellebore seeds should be sown as soon as they are ripe in May and June. Some will germinate soon, others not until the spring.

Hardy cyclamen seedlings germinate in the spring around your original plants. Prick these out into a holding area until their corms are large enough to be put into their final flowering positions.

Rosemary Verey
Gardening adviser and writer

LILIES IN WAITING

Grow the lilies you plan to bring into the house in pots, but put them out in the garden if you have to be away from home. Plunge the pots into the ground, slightly below the surface, water them well, and they will survive and be ready to take into the house when you come back.

The Lady King

ROCK THE CLEMATIS

Clematis adore the sun but their roots abhor it. How then does one persuade them to flower in a position exposed to the sun's glare? One answer is to place a slab of rock or similar on the soil above the root system. The effect on growth is often dramatic and the rock may also be used as a distributor on which to pour water during the summer.

Roy Lancaster
Horticultural consultant

PLANTING SNOWDROPS

If you are a first-time snowdrop grower, beg half a clump from a friend. Replant his half for him, nicely split, and he will be so pleased to see his crop increased you will be very welcome to have more next year.

Vanessa Courtney
Assistant producer, BBC TV

PROTECTING DAFFODILS

I love to see drifts of daffodils naturalized in the grass, but when they are just beginning to poke up their heads the little green shoots are almost invisible and it is all too easy to trample on them. We now 'mark' our drifts with snowdrops planted among the daffodils. They come up so much earlier that we can see where not to walk and it gives an extended flower season to the area.

Gordon Welburn
Head gardener

LEAVE THE LEAVES

Daffodils in the border look so lovely but when they are over they are just a nasty mess. If you cut off the leaves the bulbs won't flower next year. Instead, hide the untidy foliage by planting hostas amongst the daffodils. Their decorative leaves will come up after the daffodils and completely cover their remains.

Roddy Llewellyn
Garden designer

BUTTERFLIES IN THE GARDEN

You will enjoy seeing butterflies in your garden

throughout the summer (and sometimes in the winter months) by planting just a few nectar-rich plants – and you will enjoy the flowers too! Try these: winter-flowering heathers, aubretia, valerian, hebes, marigolds, purple buddleias, *Sedum spectabile* and Michaelmas daisies.

Ian Hardy
Butterfly conservationist

RUNNERS IN THE NEWS

Folded newspaper – it must be folded, not crumpled – in the bottom of the trench you have dug for your runner beans, covered with good compost, will ensure a super crop every time.

Field Marshal The Lord Bramall

PLENTY OF BOTTLE

To make an asparagus bed, dig a two-foot-deep trench and fill the bottom with old glass bottles. I always appear to have plenty of wine bottles. Cover the bottles with a foot of compost and plant asparagus crowns; fill the trench with earth. Apparently the roots of the asparagus like slithering round the glass bottles, which also help to keep the plants well drained.

Sir Terence Conran

POP-UP PARSLEY

Parsley is tricky to get going, but if you water the seeds regularly with quite warm water when you have sown them you will have success every time.

Mrs Robert Dean

STAGGERING THE CROP

If you hammer a nail through the stalks of some of your cauliflower and broccoli plants, those with a hole will mature earlier than those without and you will not have them all ripening at the same time.

Diana Wilson

TOPPING UP

When filling pots, tubs and other plant containers, stop about 1–2 inches from the top. Then, when watering, you can top up to the rim in the knowledge that the plants will have a good soaking with no fear of the compost being washed out.

Dr Stephan T. Buczacki
Gardening journalist and broadcaster

NEW PLANTS

It is so easy to lose a newly acquired plant after it has been planted out – it has to compete with established growth and you must remember to water it regularly. I suggest you plant it with good potting compost, in a pot much larger than it requires, and keep it near to hand so that watering is easy. Once it is strong and well established you can transfer it to its permanent home.

Jean Sambrook
The Hardy Plant Society

PLANNING A NEW BORDER

Instead of using pegs and string to mark out the shape of a new flower border, lay down a length of garden hose. Because it is flexible it produces a far more flowing curve, and if it's not quite right can easily be adjusted with a gentle kick here and there.

Vernon Russell-Smith
Garden designer

SUPPORT TIGHTS

To support a 'rocking' plant – e.g. a rose bush –
fasten it to a wooden stake with a pair of old tights,
fully extended. The stretch holds the plant secure.

Mrs Anne Abbott

… One-and-a-half-inch strips cut crosswise from
stockings or tights make excellent garden ties,
strong, elastic and soft on stalks.

Mrs Joan V. Leonardi

POT-SHOTS

The sporting way to water plants in a hanging
basket that is too high to reach is to lob ice-cubes
into it. The ice-cubes dissolve slowly so that you
won't drench anyone who walks underneath. As a
special treat, add a little liquid plant food to the
water before freezing – but be sure to mark the ice-
tray clearly or you could inadvertently poison your
husband next time he has a drink.

Lindy Harris
Industrial market researcher

SPARE THE CANE

Before hammering a bamboo cane into the
ground, fit a spent cartridge over the top. You can
then bang away to your heart's content without
splitting it.

Angela Uzielli
Ladies Open Golf Champion 1990

EYES RIGHT

A recent TV gardening programme suggested that you should use pieces of polystyrene to top garden canes, in order to avoid accidental eye injury. Old wine corks are more effective and less of another kind of eyesore.

Elizabeth Holden

… By putting a piece of white tape over the top of sharp stakes, the eye catches a flash of white and avoiding action follows almost automatically.

Duncan McEuan
Christie's wine department

QUICK, QUICK, SLOW

A rule to remember when dealing with garden pests: if it is slow-moving stamp on it; if it is fast-moving leave it alone – it will probably kill something else.

Esme Boughey
Northants organizer, National Gardens Scheme

MANNING THE BARRICADES

The snails in my Kentish garden seem to thrive on hostas. In the spring, I manage to keep them at bay by erecting a circle of horticultural grit around the plants: the leaves soon spread so that the barricades don't show. This is not a Hitler-like final solution to the little sods, but it certainly helps. So does walking round the garden at night with a flashlight and picking them up. Where you deposit them depends, rather, on your feelings about your next-door neighbours. A friend of mine freely admits to sending them off 'air mail'.

Audrey Eyton
Author of The F-Plan Diet

... Scatter broken eggshells round cherished plants: slugs do not like the rough edges. Cheaper than slug pellets this method won't kill hedgehogs and birds.

Doreen Buckingham

... Encourage hedgehogs into your garden: they will eat slugs with great enthusiasm.

Bernadette Vallely
Author of 1001 Ways to Save the Planet

MOLE CATCHING

If you're unwilling to kill moles, here is a safe and humane method of deterring them. Buy a child's 'seaside windmill' – the bigger and noisier the better. Set it in the middle of your lawn, making sure that the hole in the grass is big enough to let the 'stem' rotate to face whatever breeze is blowing. Then simply leave it *in situ*. The noise of the windmill will be anathema to the moles and they will eventually leave your garden and go to trouble someone else.

Dr David Delvin
Writer and broadcaster

ON GUARD

Try putting mothballs among your cherished plants to repel cats – mind you, three labradors do a better job!

Alan Titchmarsh
Gardening expert

NO DEER

To stop deer eating your roses, dig in some lion's dung.

Jim Gardner
Game warden, Kenya

... Human hair will keep deer away. Ask your hairdresser for sweepings, fill little muslin bags and hang them on shrubs wherever you are afraid the marauders will start guzzling.

Vernon Russell-Smith
Garden designer

WARDING OFF GREENFLY

Bury cloves of garlic at the foot of your rose bushes to ward off greenfly. You may find you have planted garlic, in which case you will have even fewer greenfly and more garlic.

Diana, Lady Avebury
Literary agent

GET NETTLED

To deter whitefly, cut lots of nettles, put them into a big plastic container and cover them with water. Leave them in the sun for three days; then strain off the resulting liquid and dilute it with water – about five pints of water to one of the liquid. Spray this wherever it is needed. An added bonus: any liquid and rotted nettles left over make a wonderful fertilizer.

HIRH Archduchess Helen of Hapsburg

FLY AWAY

Sow summer savory in between broad beans to prevent attacks by blackfly. Plant small-flowered *Tagetes* (French marigolds) between tomatoes to ward off whitefly.

Alan Titchmarsh
Gardening expert

MONEYSPINNER

You can make an economical and green-minded pest spray for your roses by whirling up all your old soap ends in a liquidizer with lots of water.

Mrs Charles Shepley-Cuthbert

MAKE IT STICK

When spraying roses against pests, add a few drops of washing-up liquid to the mixture. This will help the spray to stick to the leaves rather than running off like raindrops.

H. R. Herrington
Managing director, Alcan

BANNING THE BINDWEED

You can't get rid of bindweed by digging it up. The only way is to spray the leaves with weedkiller and wait for it to be absorbed back to the roots. This is easier said than done without also killing off the plant to which it is attached, but this is my way: Unwind the bindweed from the plant, stuff the trails into a plastic bag, and squirt in the weedkiller. The bag will protect the other plants while you wait patiently for the weedkiller to do its work.

Alternatively, wearing fabric gloves over rubber ones (to keep the weedkiller off your skin), dip your hands into the weedkiller and draw them gently up the bindweed, taking care not to touch other plants.

Dr Anthony Russell
Bishop of Dorchester

HANDY SPRAYS

Fill a pint-sized house-plant sprayer with a solution of Tumbleweed or Roundup, and keep it handy. It is then no effort to deal with isolated appearances of bindweed or ground elder. Likewise, fill a second sprayer with green-or whitefly killer.

The Hon. Lady Butler

SUNBATHING LAWN

Anyone who wants a patch of lawn on which to sunbathe but doesn't want the chore of mowing yards of turf might consider making a green catafalque. This is a free-standing rectangular raised bed of approximately 7 feet by 3 feet, held within an attractive stone or brick wall 30 inches high. Half filled with hard core and gravel and topped off with a decant loam, this bed can be sown with a good fine grass lawn seed mixture.

The resultant lawn could almost be mown in half and hour with a pair of nail clippers. Friends can be told it is the tomb of an early local prince and its sides can be decorated with trailing plants like lobelia or other pretty wall-dwellers like Cheddar pinks set in holes provided for the purpose.

Graham Rose
Gardening correspondent

CAMPHOR CURE

Many prunuses are subject to leaf curl and the one in our garden was struck every year. On the advice of a knowledgeable friend we strung camphor rings about its branches and it hasn't been troubled since by this problem.

H H Judge Fox-Andrews

TURF IT

If your garden is getting out of control and causing panic, invest in some turves and turf all the flowerbeds but one. Plant for colour and mow the rest of the area.

Richard Briers
Actor

RUST-FREE

Keep small garden tools rust-free by storing them in a bucket of oiled sand.

Valerie Moyses

IN FOR A DIP

Few people seem to cut their hedges with good old-fashioned shears any more. I'm one of a dying breed, but when I took mine to our village shop to be sharpened, the old boy there said categorically: 'Shears *never* go blunt.' I thought he had gone off his rocker until he explained that shears don't have sharp blades like a knife. They are more like scissors, and it's the build-up of sap that forces the blades apart. 'All you need to do,' he said, 'is to keep a bucket of soapy water by you, and dip in the blades every tenth cut.' And he's perfectly right.

Donald Sinden
Actor

CLEAN HANDS

To clean hands after gardening, or doing the flowers, rub them with a mixture of lemon juice, granulated sugar and olive oil. This is tremendously successful.

The Hon. Mrs Charles Kitchener

GLOVE TRICK

Whenever you are wearing gardening gloves or rubber gloves, cover your hands with cream and let it really soak in while you work.

Sue Lawley
TV presenter

A LITTLE LIGHT MUSIC

A new discovery for me: gardening with a Walkman has changed my life!

Frederick Fox
Milliner

IN THE LAUNDRY

They that wash on Monday
Have all the week to dry;
They that wash on Tuesday
Are not so much awry;
They that wash on Wednesday
Are not so much to blame;
They that wash on Thursday
Wash for shame;
They that wash on Friday
Wash in need;
And they that wash on Saturday,
Oh! they're sluts indeed.

ANON.

A STICKY BUSINESS

To remove chewing-gum from clothes, place the garment in the freezer overnight. The following day the chewing-gum can easily be scraped off. The same principle applies to gum on the carpet. Rub it with an ice cube until the gum is solid and then chip it away.

Will Pease
Undergraduate

SPIT IT OUT

If you prick yourself when sewing cotton or silk and get blood on the fabric the best way to remove it is with saliva. Spit on a knot of cotton thread and dab it on the mark – this will not only get rid of the blood but also prevents iron mould developing. N.B. Your saliva will only work on your own blood.

Christine Hancock
Royal College of Nursing

UNDERCOVER AGENT

Vinegar will help to remove underarm perspiration stains, especially on coloured fabric.

Peggy Smith
RADA wardrobe department

BACK TO WHITE

You can get the stains out of white socks by adding bicarbonate of soda liberally while washing. And grass stains can be removed from cotton fabrics, such as cricket whites, by rubbing them with neat methylated spirits.

June Zetter
Mother of six

POLLEN COUNT

Should you get pollen on your clothes when arranging lilies etc. *don't* try to brush it off. Simply remove it with sticky tape.

The Lady Fanshawe

A GOOD SOAK

If you get a stain on a garment that resists

lukewarm water and soap, try soaking it overnight in a bucket of cold water. This sounds ridiculous, but you will be surprised how often you will find no stain in the morning.

Shirley Conran
Writer

SPRAY AWAY

Squirt hairspray directly on to an ink stain from about three inches away. Rub the stain gently with a hidden section of the garment, rinse it with cold water and repeat, if necessary. This works on leather too, but rub it with a soft cloth.

Tessa Dahl
Writer

ON YOUR MARKS

To clean stains or spots: rub the mark with an ice cube. David (Lord Perth) suggested spraying soda water on the place. That seems excessive if you are in the dress!

The Countess of Perth

FOR MESSY EATERS

When, at a meal, soup or food gets on a tie, soak it well with dry white wine – this usually takes the stain out.

The Rt. Hon. The Lord Havers

… For spillage of soup or spaghetti sauce on a tie or silk blouse, shake talcum powder on to the stain, leave it for five minutes and then brush it off.

The Lord White
Chairman, Hanson Industries

... Spanish restaurants always keep a tin of talc for 'messy eaters'. Grease spots and even coffee stains are dusted with talcum powder, brushed off later, and the guest leaves clean.

Mrs Miguel Ferrer

OUT, DAMNED SPOT

After removing a stain it helps to avoid a ring if you dry the spot quickly with a hairdrier.

Dorothy Parker

HANDKERCHIEF CRISES

When your gentleman caller spills some drink and uses his handkerchief to wipe it up, rinse out the handkerchief and flatten it with your hands on your bathroom mirror. Assuming he has come for the evening, the handkerchief will have time to dry. Peel it from the mirror, and it will look freshly ironed. Fold neatly and when you hand it back to him he'll be frightfully impressed.

Susan Crosland
Columnist

ROLLING AWAY

When I want to clean velvet I wrap Sellotape, sticky side out, round a jamjar. I lay the velvet garment out flat and roll the sticky jamjar over it. All the little bits come away on it.

Mrs Michael Heseltine

... To remove cat hairs from my clothes I wrap sticky tape around my hand, sticky side out.

Andrea Newman
Writer

TALLY HO!

To clean a pair of riding or hunting boots, first wash and scrub them with cold water, rub them down and leave them until they're completely dry. Then apply black shoe polish moistened with vinegar, and bone them thoroughly with a dry deer bone: this is done by using both hands on the bone and pulling it vigorously up and down the surfaces of the boot. Brush the boots with a clean brush and polish them with a clean cloth. Result: a gleaming surface.

To get a really good gloss on a black top hat, hunting or ceremonial, first wash off the mud and dirt with a stiff brush dipped in cold water. Then sponge it down in the direction of the nap. Now apply a solution of two-thirds methylated spirits and one-third water, used sparingly and sponged carefully with the nap. Allow the hat to dry and finish by polishing it with an old stocking. An alternative solution for the final polish is brown ale.

Michael Clayton
Editor, Horse and Hound

MELTING MOMENTS

Invariably, when a tin of shoe polish is half used up, it starts to crack and dry out. Put the tin on a low heat for a few minutes until the polish has melted back to a nice even cream, and when it is cool it will be as good as new.

Tony Slater
Management consultant

SHINE ON

To make black patent shoes really shine, rub them lightly with Vaseline.

Charlotte de Rothschild
Concert singer

SHOE-SHINE BOY

If leather shoes are really scuffed, rub them over with the cut half of a potato before polishing.

Sir Michael Hordern
Actor

IN THE BAG

To avoid getting white stuff all over your hands when cleaning white sandals, first put the hand that goes inside the shoe in a plastic bag.

Beth Williams

A CLEAN SWEEP

Most people don't realize that if you want to clean a white or pastel felt hat you should never attempt to do it with a liquid drycleaner. Inevitably this will make rings that you won't be able to get out. Rub it instead with the very finest sandpaper.

Frederick Fox
Milliner

STUBBORNEST SPOTS

If you are ecologically minded and have changed over to Ecover washing-up liquid but don't know what to do with your old washing-up liquid, don't fret. Use it on the stubbornest grease spots before putting the garments into the washing machine. Put a concentrated drop on the spot, leave it for a few seconds, rinse it with cold water and put the item in the wash. This has never failed to work for me.

Anna Massey
Actress

UNCREASED SHEETS

Loosely fold drip-dry sheets before putting them

into the washing machine and they will come out almost uncreased.

The Hon. Lady Butler

COVER CO-ORDINATION

Wash and iron duvet covers inside out. Then put your arms into the top inside corners and take hold of the top corners of the duvet through the cover. Shake well until the duvet cover falls correctly over the duvet.

Mrs Nigel Talbot-Rice

TANGLE-FREE WASHING

When washing tights or jumpers in the machine, put them in a pillowcase. This helps to keep the jumpers soft and the tights from tangling round the other washing.

Frances A. Fox
The National Housewives' Association

FOIL THE FLOOD

If your washing machine breaks down when it's full of clothes and soapy water, lift out the waste hose and drop it down to let the water drain into a large low basin – then you can open the door safely.

Jim Collins
Butler

PUFFED UP

If you are putting wet padded clothing or pillows – feather or fibre-filled – into the tumbledrier, add a tennis ball. This acts as a 'puffer-upper' and helps to distribute the fillings more evenly.

Cheryl Rose

NO-RINSE WOOL

For a sure-fire no-shrink wool wash, mix together in a large screw-topped jar one cup of methylated spirits, one cup of Lux flakes and a small bottle of eucalyptus oil. Add one tablespoon of this mixture to a bucket of warm water. Wash the woollies in the bucket but don't rinse them; just give them a gentle spin and dry them in the normal way.

Diana Wilson

FLAT OUT

How do you dry woollies in a small house or flat? I first roll them in a towel, then spread them flat on wadges of newspaper on the carpet. Pale-coloured jumpers and cardis, which might get newsprint on them, should be laid on a towel on top of the paper. Warning: keep pussy-cats out. They love to snuggle onto nice, clean, soft woollies.

Marjorie Proops
Agony aunt

SIMPLY FREEZING

Cotton and silk are best ironed slightly damp but so often the ironing has just reached the perfect state when you are too busy to tackle it. When this happens, pop it all into a polythene bag, tie it up and put it in the freezer. It will stay in just the right condition until you are ready. Two or three minutes is all you need to shake it out and start dashing away with the smoothing iron.

Cathy Pennock
Stockbroker

DAMPING DOWN

If the laundry has dried out too much, sprinkle it liberally with cold water and put it, in a plastic bag, into the fridge. Leave it for half an hour, and when you take it out the dampness will be evenly distributed and your ironing easier to accomplish.

Eleanor Bron
Actress and writer

LETTING OFF STEAM

I use a plant spray when ironing. The mist of water gives a better steaming effect (and better finish) than an iron's built-in spray, which I find often leaves uneven wet patches on the clothes.

Elizabeth Tilberis

PRESS ON

When faced with a pile of ironing, switch on *The Archers* and see how much you can get done before somebody says, 'Oh Tony, honestly!'

Victoria Wood
Comedienne

THE TOWEL TECHNIQUE

Embroidered table mats – or any embroidery or appliqué – are much easier to iron if you put a terry towel on the ironing board and iron them on that. Very special things should really be ironed through tissue paper, or better still, through dampened cotton cambric.

Mrs Richard Westmacott

SKIRTING THE PROBLEM

The best way to iron the pleats of a skirt is to turn it inside out and press firmly over dampened brown paper. But be sure to use the dull not the shiny side.

Roland Klein
Fashion designer

SHIRT TALES

Try a different way to iron a shirt. Press the sleeves and collar first as usual. Then iron the *inside* of the back. Fold one side up on to the back and iron that, and do the same to the other side. Hey presto, shirt ironed. I do one shirt the old way, another this way, timing myself to see which is quickest. I haven't proved anything but it certainly concentrates the mind.

June Zetter
Mother of six

WAX POLISH

If you rub the end of a candle over the base of the iron after you have switched it off – i.e. when it is still warm but not very – and then give it a good rub with kitchen paper, it will be really clean for the next session.

Mrs Gordon Welburn

CLEANING

Cleaning your house while your kids are still growing
Is like shovelling the walk before it stops snowing.

PHYLLIS DILLER

KITCHEN THINGS

TACKY SALAD BOWLS

Dressings with oil in them make wooden salad bowls very sticky. Don't wash them: mix a little lemon juice with a few drops of olive oil and work it well into the wood with a cotton cloth. Wipe off with a clean cloth, polishing hard as you go.

Maria Montes-Riveiro
Spanish daily

TASTELESS

Rubbing a chopping board with cut lemon will remove the taste of onions and garlic – and also whiten it if it is discoloured.

Kate Thompson
Norland nanny

STAINED TEACUPS

Brown stains inside teacups can easily be removed by rubbing them with salt.

Mrs Colin Franklin

THE FULL FLAVOUR

Old, dark tea stains in the pot really do spoil the flavour. Keep the pot clean and sweet by putting in two dessertspoons of bicarbonate of soda, filling it up with boiling water, and leaving it to soak for a couple of hours. Rinse out the pot with fresh water before using it. Or you could use a tablet of Steradent (denture cleaner), in which case use cold water instead of hot.

Sam Twining

… Steradent is a good cleaner for thermos flasks.

Mrs Tom Cochrane

A CLEAN SHAVE

Use a disposable razor to scrape dirt off the glass door of your cooker. It works like magic.

Esme Boughey
Northants organizer, National Gardens Scheme

OVEN READY

Mix a tablespoonful of bicarbonate of soda with a pint of boiling water (watch out, it froths a lot) and keep it in a screw-topped jar. When the oven is warm, paint it with the mixture and let it dry. The coating will keep the oven clean. Wipe it down after a month or two and paint again.

Anne Morrison
Foster-mother

WHAT A WASTE!

If the waste disposer gets clogged with grease, it is sometimes possible to clear it by dropping down some ice cubes – no water – and letting it grind them up.

Tom Cochrane
Plumber

SELF-CLEANING

If you find it a fiddle to wash your liquidizer by hand, and that it is an awkward space-eater in the dishwasher, let it clean itself. Pour in some hot water and one drop of washing-up liquid, and whizz. Change the water and you have an instant rinse too.

Elizabeth Holden

MAKE IT YOURSELF

Dishwasher powders contain very strong chemicals. Make your own for light washes with one part borax to two parts baking soda.

Bernadette Vallely
Author of 1001 Ways to Save the Planet

SCALE AWAY

A repairman who charged me a great deal to mend my scaled-up dishwasher told me this. To get rid of scale (and thus save the motor), throw some powdered vitamin C, bought at the chemist, into the machine and run it through on the normal cycle. If you also administer vitamin C to yourself you may prevent time-consuming winter colds.

Jonathan Dimbleby
TV news commentator

CARAMEL-COATED

It is surprising that the pan in which you have cooked caramel is more easily cleaned by soaking in cold water than hot.

Lee Alfandary
School secretary

THE SAKI SOLUTION

Pour some saki (Japanese rice beer) into a stained saucepan and heat it almost to boiling point. When you pour off the saki, the saucepan will be free of stain. N.B. Don't drink the saki.

Sir Kingsley Amis
Author

BLAST OFF

Here's a tip for burnt saucepans – and I mean burnt! For a two-pint saucepan, take a teacup of any biological washing powder and spread it over the burnt surface. Add two teacups of water to cover, and simmer gently for about ten minutes. Pour the contents away and then, using a stiff washing-up brush, clean the pan. If this doesn't completely lift the burnt material, repeat the process.

Jan Leeming
TV presenter

PUT OUT TO GRASS

If an oven dish gets burnt, put it face downwards on the grass all night: next morning it will easily wash clean.

Field Marshal The Lord Bramall

GOOD NEWS

To brighten a stainless steel sink, polish it with newspaper.

Field Marshal Sir Ruthven Wade

... To bring up your copper shining bright, wipe it over with a well-soaked page of newsprint (preferably from a tabloid) and polish it with a linen rag.

Lady Audley

COPPER PANS

When I married Terence some twenty years ago he had the most wonderful collection of copper cooking pans which I realized I was to be responsible for cleaning. After much thought I remembered cleaning my brass Brownie badge with lemon juice and salt. To this day I use a teaspoon of each to clean the saucepans every time I use them. They don't shine and glint the way they would if properly cleaned but they certainly look spotless and untarnished – and this process takes only a minute.

Mrs Terence Donovan

FURRY KETTLES

To get rid of the build-up of lime scale inside a kettle, fill the kettle with equal parts of vinegar and water; bring it to the boil and let it stand overnight. Alternatively, fill the kettle with water and freeze it for about six hours. The lime is worked free by the cold, and when the water melts it will bring out the scale with it.

Glenys Kinnock

PRECIOUS THINGS

SALT FOR SILK FLOWERS

Artificial silk flowers can be cleaned with salt. Put them head first, stems projecting, into a pillowcase or bin liner and pour in a pound of salt, tying the top tightly. Shake the case for a minute or two to make sure that the flowers and salt are well mixed. Remove the flowers, blow away any grains of salt adhering to them and they will be as good as new.

Mrs Roy Dotrice

VELLUM BINDINGS

An old book in a vellum binding can be a treasure and must be cleaned with great care. Dip a pad of cotton wool in milk and rub the vellum very gently in little circles, a small section at a time. You will be amazed at the amount of dirt that comes off. Finally, rub the binding with a clean cloth.

Anthony Rainbird
Director, SSZ Bookbinders

SPITTING IMAGE

To clean the surface of an oil painting, spit on it and rub gently with cotton wool in circular movements.

Mrs Francis Sitwell

A GOOD SOAK

Your pearls will be very grateful if, every now and then, you give them a bath in olive oil and then polish them with a soft cloth.

Lady Georgina Coleridge
Journalist and writer

SPARKLING RINGS

Rings set with precious stones get amazingly dirty, sometimes without one noticing. All they need is to be gently scrubbed with a soft toothbrush in hot water and detergent, rinsed, dried and finally dipped in surgical spirit to eliminate any smears.

Raymond Sancroft-Baker
Christie's jewellery department

POLISHED THINGS

A CLEAR VIEW

To make your windows really shine, clean them with wet newspaper, then polish them with a soft cloth.

Dame Judi Dench
Actress

SMEAR-FREE

Much cheaper than bought window-cleaner and just as effective is a mixture of one part methylated spirits, one part paraffin oil and one part water. Put it into a litre bottle and shake it well before applying, very sparingly, with a soft cloth to windows or mirrors. Rub up with a clean duster for a long-lasting smear-free finish.

Dorothy Davies

CLEANING DECANTERS

Drop two Steradent tablets into a decanter filled with hot water and leave it for an hour. If the bottom of the decanter is very dirty add shot from a cartridge and swill it round the bottom.

Rosemary, Marchioness of Northampton

... I clean a decanter by putting in pieces of chopped raw potato and leaving it overnight.

Roddy Llewelyn
Garden designer

DRYING DECANTERS

To dry the inside of a decanter, first fill it to the brim with cold water, then turn it upside down and run hot water (as hot as possible) over the base while the cold water runs out. Wipe the neck of the decanter, and if there is a hint of damp left inside, give it a blast up the spout with a hairdrier.

Mrs Ivo Reid

BOTTOMS UP

You need no longer dry your drinking glasses. Put a

drying-up cloth on a flat surface and leave your glasses standing upside down on it. They will look as if they've been polished for hours.

George Baker
Actor and cook

HARD LINES

Lime lines on glass or china can easily be removed by rubbing them gently with a soft rag soaked in cider vinegar. For a really stubborn line, leave the vessel soaking in a cider vinegar solution overnight.

Mary Hodge
Royal College of Physicians

SAUCE FOR THE BRASS

My door knocker sometimes gets forgotten and looks awful – dull and tarnished. When this happens I smother it in brown sauce and leave it for five or ten minutes. Then I wash it off and all the tarnish will have gone. All it needs then is a brisk rub with Brasso to give it a shine. N.B. I use A1. but any sauce will do.

Paul Eddington
Actor

BUSTING OUT

Always resist the temptation to clean that bronze bust or nice little Renaissance statuette with metal polish, which will remove the precious patina. Instead, wash it with warm soapy water and rub it up with brown shoe polish.

James Price
Libel barrister

TOOTHBRUSH TRICK

When I'm cleaning silver and have to use a toothbrush to get right into the corners, I put a soft cloth over the bristles to stop them scratching.

Sharon Maughan
Actress

DIP IT IN

To restore egg-stained teaspoons and forks to their pristine condition, soak them in a mixture of salt, water and clean milk-bottle tops in a small jam jar.

Louise Botting
Presenter, Money Box

DECIDEDLY FISHY

A tablespoon of vinegar in the washing-up water removes fishy smells from china and cutlery.

Sandra Price
School dinner-lady

SHINE ON

To keep a good shine, always dry silver with a soft cloth (an old piece of towelling is ideal) impregnated with plate powder. Mix the powder with methylated spirits or water to a milky consistency; steep the towel in this and hang it out to drip-dry on the line. When the towel is dry, give it a good shake to get rid of surplus powder and it is then ready for use. Plate powder is very difficult to buy nowadays, but can be ordered direct from Town Talk, Slater Lane, Bolton, BL1 2TQ.

Mrs Michael Hughes-Hallett

STORING SILVER

To minimize silver cleaning, put the individual pieces you use infrequently in see-through plastic bags and tie them with twist-strips to keep the air out. Large sizes will accommodate most dishes

Susan Crosland
Columnist

EFFORTLESS

To clean tarnished silver without any effort at all, you require a plastic bowl lined with cooking foil, *very* hot water and a heaped tablespoon of Calgon, the water softener. Place your silver in the bowl so that each piece touches the foil (larger pieces need to be turned after two or three minutes so that they are 'done' all over). In a few minutes your silver will be clean.

Elizabeth Tyler-Janes

FURNISHINGS

GETTING RID OF SCRATCHES

To disguise small scratches or marks on polished furniture, crack a Brazil nut and break it in half. Rub the white part of the nut well into the scratch. The oil stains the wood and hides the scratch. Polish the wood afterwards.

Lady Owen

A GOOD SHINE

An old hospital trick that works wonders on those hideous white rings that appear on furniture after a hot mug has been put down on the polished surface: rub a little Friars' Balsam very gently into the heat mark with cotton wool, spreading well on each side of the white ring. Use more Friars' Balsam if you need it, until the ring vanishes. Lavishly polish the furniture with beeswax polish and no one will ever know the stain was there.

Claire Rayner
Novelist and agony aunt

FULL MARKS

If you have made a mark on a piece of wooden furniture (for example, a watermark), mix some cigarette ash with some olive oil until it forms a paste. Spread this over the mark generously and leave it overnight. Next day the mark should have disappeared.

The Rt. Hon. The Earl of Gowrie
Chairman, Sotheby's

To remove alcohol stains left by wet glasses on highly polished tables, gently rub in Brasso, and leave it to dry before polishing it off. Brasso can also be used to restore tortoiseshell to its original patina.

The Lord Sackville

CLEAN CANE

Willow, cane and bamboo furniture can be washed with a mixture of 125g/4oz salt, 1 tablespoon of baking soda and a quart of water. Rinse well, dry, and rub gently with linseed oil.

Kate Thompson
Norland nanny

UP IN ARMS

To DIY dryclean material on the arms of a chair (or anywhere else) use the crust of a loaf of bread like an India rubber, dough-side down on the cloth. It makes a fearful mess but it is effective.

David Hicks
Interior decorator

FOAM OFF

Foamy shaving cream works as a spot-remover on upholstery and carpets. Spread some on the mark, let it dry and then brush it off.

The Rt. Hon. Sir David Steel
MP

BIRD BATH

When a bird that had feasted on elderberries got into my spare bedroom, the resulting devastation to pale pink bedspreads and wallpaper can only be imagined. However, it all came out with white wine.

The Lady Fanshawe

ON THE CARPET

Cold water and cotton wool is all you need to get almost any dirty mark out of a carpet. Just rub briskly with the wet cotton wool – the friction does the trick.

Carolyn MacKenzie
Freelance book editor

SCORCHED!

If your log fire spits and the embers leave black marks on the carpet, rub them with a copper coin and the mark will disappear. This is best done as soon as possible.

The Lady Carrington

RED WINE SPILLS

If red wine gets dropped on the carpet, pour white wine on to it immediately, and leave it for five or ten minutes before mopping it up.

HRH The Princess Margaret, Countess of Snowdon

WAX AWAY

Candle wax that has dripped on to a tablecloth can be removed by covering the spillage with brown paper or blotting paper and pressing it with a hot iron. The wax will stick to the paper and leave the cloth clean.

Christian, Lady Hesketh

... To take candle wax off polished surfaces, cover it with a piece of brown wrapping paper, folded several times, and press it gently with a very cool iron. N.B. It is unwise to use blotting paper for this.

The Duchess of Marlborough

ABOUT THE HOUSE

*I make no secret of the fact that I would rather lie on
a sofa than sweep beneath it. But you have to be
efficient if you're going to be lazy.*

SHIRLEY CONRAN

MOVING HOUSE

When moving house, leave behind for your
successors the names and addresses of any suppliers
or contractors you have used recently, so that they
know who to contact in case of problems. Also
pass on the names of reliable window-cleaners,
painters and decorators, mini-cab firms, etc. And
don't forget to ask for a similar list from the people
whose house you are buying.

The Rt. Hon. William Rodgers
Director General, RIBA

LIGHTER LATER

When shifting things around the house, move the
heavy items first; then the task becomes
progressively easier.

Stephen Massey
Christie's New York

TAPE IT

When shopping for furniture, be sure to take a tape measure and details of room sizes. Everything looks so much smaller in a large store than it does at home. And never buy a bed when you're tired. *Any* bed will feel comfortable then.

Tina Fotherby
British Home Furnishing Bureau

TURNING THE TABLES

Card tables have many uses, not least as extra dining tables. Two pushed together and covered with a floor-length cloth not only look attractive but are a very accommodating size – and they stack away easily afterwards. A good idea for young couples just setting up home – or anywhere space is limited.

Mrs Kenneth Evans

MIRROR, MIRROR

Mirrors make all the difference to the look of a room, but good ones can be hideously expensive. An alternative is to scour junk shops for antique picture frames, and have mirror glass cut to fit them.

Ann Boanas
Antique collector

ALL THINGS NICE

I always keep an old spice cabinet within reach of my studio desk. It presents me with eight transparent scoops, four large and four small, each with a carrying handle. Mine holds my office supplies – rubber bands, paper clips, drawing pins, paper fasteners, indicator pins, staples, bulldog clips and ring reinforcements –

but it could store anything small, from sewing materials to make-up.

Dorothy Dunnett
Author

KEEPING A RECORD

Whenever you're furnishing a room, clip together swatches of the wallpaper, carpet, fabrics and paint colours, each clearly marked with the manufacturer's name, reference number and so on. This is essential for colour-matching lamps and cushions, and extremely useful if you want to re-order anything later on.

Jill Melford
Actress

STEP-BY-STEP

When ordering a stair carpet, buy half a yard more than you need. Fold this extra piece under the bottom step, and each time the edges of the tread start to wear the carpet can be moved up three inches.

Peter Watts
Professional carpet-layer

SEEING THE LIGHT

If you want to avoid the dreaded net curtain but don't want to be overlooked, get a reputable blind-making company to process voile, muslin or some similar fabric (preferably one with a slub) and turn it into a roller blind. You can then, if you like, finish it off with a fine fan edging along the bottom.

Lavinia Dargie
Interior designer

ONE-WAY WINDOWS

If you are without curtains while moving or decorating and don't want the neighbours peering in, paint the windows with a thin solution of beer and flour. You will be able to see out but a passer-by won't see in.

Stephanie Bueltemann

ECONOMY MEASURES

Use sheets for curtains – some of the American ones are particularly pretty.

Use felt for curtains – it doesn't have to be lined.

Use dyed muslin for curtains – gather it up very fully.

Use thick felt as a stand-by floor covering – it can be covered with rugs.

Sara Allday
Interior designer

OVER YOUR SHOULDER

When hanging curtains, always bundle them on your left shoulder, which makes it easier when you carry them up the ladder. I've done this many times over the years and it really does make the job easier.

Odette Hallowes
Wartime heroine

SMOOTH RUNNING

A little wax polish or Vaseline rubbed along a curtain rail will make the curtains pull across easily.

Dora Saint
'Miss Read', author

NON-STICK BULBS

A dab of Vaseline applied with a fingertip to the grooves of a light bulb will stop it sticking in the socket when you come to change it.

J. M. Edelstein
Senior bibliographer, Getty Center, Los Angeles

A LONG LIFE

If you use dimmers on your light switches, so that when you turn on the lights they come on slowly, you will find that your bulbs will sometimes last literally for years. It is the sudden snapping on to full power that ages the bulbs. You will pay yourself back for the original cost in a matter of months.

Elizabeth Jane Howard
Novelist

FLATTERING

You can make a sparsely furnished room look wonderful at night, simply by using candlelight. Once lit, the effect of a mass of strategically placed candles – including nightlights – grouped together in holders of different shapes and heights, is sensational.

Laurie Purden
Journalist

A SNUG FIT

If your candle is the wrong size for your candlestick, dunk the bottom inch or so in very hot water. When the wax is soft, squidge the candle instantly into the holder.

Frank Morgan
Churchwarden

FROZEN CANDLES

To prevent candles from dripping, pop them into the deep freeze. Frozen wax burns too slowly to drip and it is economical, too, as they burn much more slowly and so last longer.

HRH Princess Michael of Kent

MOTHS AWAY

Put the ends of your bath soaps in clothes cupboards and drawers. They keep the moths at bay and make everything smell nice.

Michael Mander

... Conkers placed in wardrobes or cupboard drawers will keep moths away.

Mrs Iain Campbell-Blair

FLY AWAY

A large bunch of mint in the kitchen helps to keep away the flies.

Sprays of eucalyptus are also an aid to warding them off, and look more decorative in other rooms.

Dame Judi Dench
Actress

... A scented-leaf geranium plant will ensure there are no flies in your kitchen.

Brenda Hawkins
RADA wardrobe department

SWEET SICK ROOM

Keep a bowl of vinegar and water in the sick room. It freshens the air and keeps it sweet.

Kate Thompson
Norland nanny

MUST

Two or three spots of vanilla essence in the back corner of a drawer or wardrobe will get rid of a musty smell.

Noelle Walsh

CLEAR THE AIR

Lighting a match and allowing it to burn down is a good way of removing smells in the loo.

Bryan Gould
MP

THE MORNING AFTER

If a room smells of stale cigarette smoke, a wet sponge on a plate will absorb it.

Roland Klein
Fashion designer

PAINT SMELLS

If you are heartily sick of the smell of paint by the time you have finished decorating, you can easily get rid of it by leaving the cut halves of an onion on a saucer in the middle of the room – and no, the room won't reek of onion in the morning.

Sandra Hendley

A GOOD BLOW

Quite apart from drying your hair, a hairdrier will dry cake tins which are inclined to rust if there is a hint of damp left after washing; get a good blaze going in an open fire; defrost a frozen pipe, and dry the inside of wellington boots.

Various

DRIP GUARD

Spray Scotchguard on the carpet around the loo as splash protection against careless operators.

Michael Mander

NEW LIFE FOR OLD BATHS

Old baths and basins sometimes have hideous dark green stains where water has dripped over the years. Before having our bath re-enamelled we gave it a last chance and rubbed the stains with Steradent. Amazing! The stains went away and what's more, they haven't come back.

Emma Fellowes
Private secretary to HRH Princess Michael of Kent

PROTECTING PRECIOUS ORNAMENTS

Stick precious ornaments down with Blu-Tack to prevent breakages when dusting.

The Lady Hereford

PILE UP

If after moving furniture you find indents in the carpet, put an ice cube on each one, leave it to melt and the pile will spring up again.

The Lady Fanshawe

WASTED EFFORT

Never carry your wastepaper baskets to the bin, one by one. Take a dustbin liner round the house and fill it up as you go. It saves ages!

Mrs Michael Hughes-Hallett

SAGGY SEATS

When cane chairs sag, sponge them with hot, strongly salted water. Stand them in a draught to dry, and do not use for a day or two.

from *Aunt Daisy's New Zealand scrap-book*

HAND IN GLOVE

To clean Venetian blinds and louvred doors put on fabric gloves and dip your hands into hot soapy water. It is easy to draw your fingers along each strip, washing as you go.

Mrs Tom Cochrane

A COLD START

If you run cold water into the bath first, you will not get as steamy a bath as when you start with hot water, however hot the final bath.

Sheila Black
Journalist

ADVICE TO NEWLYWEDS

Never keep up with the Joneses. Drag them down to your level; it's cheaper.

The Rt. Rev. Mervyn Stockwood

FLOWERS IN THE HOUSE

Doing the flowers
Takes hours.
And when they're done,
They're done.
Still, it's fun.

ANON.

THE PENCIL TEST

When watering pot plants, stick a pencil in the earth at the side of the pot. If it comes up clean the plant needs water.

The Lady Hereford

A GOOD SOAK

Stop an azalea from flagging by submerging the pot once a week in a bucket of water. Leave it there until the bubbles have subsided and drain it well before putting it back. Of course, azaleas like rain water best but they must make the best of what they can get, like the rest of us.

The Lord Porchester

CYCLAMEN FOR ANOTHER YEAR

So many people throw out their indoor cyclamen plants, when with a little care they will go on for years increasing in size. When they have finished flowering keep them frost-free and not too damp. At the end of May put them out under a north wall and leave them to mature – no water other than rain (the drier the summer the better – they really like to be baked, which is what happens to them in the wild). At the end of September bring them indoors, and with feed and water, they should flower again.

Mrs John Hawkesworth

SPLIT-LEVEL PLANTING

There is a way of getting a more dense flowering of potted tulips. This is by planting them at two different levels in the pot. Even those at the bottom will emerge happily, having wound their way to the surface between the bulbs planted above them.

Sir Nicholas Henderson
Former ambassador to Washington

HEADS HIGH

When given a bunch of tulips, pierce each stem just below the flower with a pin to make a hole, and they will remain fresh and upright for much longer.

Lynda Lee-Potter
Columnist, Daily Mail

ALL TOGETHER

Cut the heads off tulips when they are partly open and arrange them, tightly packed, like chocolates, in a shallow bowl.

Conchita Naviero
Spanish daily

GOING UNDER

Delicately stemmed violets often look weak and tired when you first buy them. Completely submerging them in a bowl of water for a couple of hours – no more – will revitalize them.

Jane Packer
Floral designer

PARTY PEONIES

Peonies are best bought in bud, but if you want them to look wonderful the same day submerge them in hot water right up to their necks for at least twenty minutes to bring them out. Pour the water away and repeat the process if necessary.

Catarina Birchell

BRINGING ON A BLUSH

Some white flowers, particularly the little white pom-pom *Achillea ptarnuco* 'The Pearl', can be tinted pink if you stand them overnight in deep water to which you have added cochineal.

Judith Baker
Nursery gardener

FLOWER POWER

If your roses hang their heads, re-cut and split the

stems, and place them in about an inch of boiling water for fifteen minutes. Then re-arrange them in warm water, and all should be well!

Lady Pulbrook

NEVER SAY DIE!

I hate throwing away bouquets I have been given and always take cuttings from them if I can. Carnations in particular seem to take easily, and do very well in town. Just nip off suitable side shoots and plant them round the edges of a pot – my roof garden is full of them, and they are doing fine!

Lady Georgina Coleridge
Journalist and author

THE KINDEST CUT

As soon as you get them, crush the bottom inch of all cut flowers and leave them standing overnight in water in a deep narrow bucket (most easily found in a DIY shop) before arranging them. Flower shops do this religiously, and it really is worth the trouble because they last twice as long.

Mrs Charles Parnell

KEEPING THE WATER FRESH

A few drops of Milton (a disinfectant) added to the water in your flower vase will stop it from smelling. So will a teaspoon of sugar, or a few drops of liquid bleach. Removing all the leaves from below the water line also helps to keep the water sweet.

Various

A BOTTLE OF FIZZ

Fizzy lemonade – about one-third of a pint of lemonade mixed with two-thirds of a pint of water – will keep carnations and pinks going for weeks.

The Hon. Lady Butler

MAKING THE MOST OF IT

When fresh flowers are scarce and you want to make a few blooms go a long way, divide them between three containers of different heights and sizes, and place them all together in a tight group so that they're almost touching. Glass looks particularly pretty – a decanter, say, against a medium-sized goblet and a tiny posy vase.

Anon.

AN IMPRESSIVE ARRANGEMENT

When making a plant display against a wall, stagger the heights by standing the taller plants for the back on up-turned plastic flower pots within the large container. Trailing plants for the front and sides can be put in at angles and all pots, gaps and earth covered with a thick layer of moss.

The Lady Hereford

STEMS TOO SHORT?

It's infuriating, in the middle of doing a complicated arrangement, to find that some of the blooms are too short to achieve the 'balance' you're after. But, providing the stems are not too thick, I find I can get around this by pushing them into drinking straws. They still get water, and I can cut them to just the right height.

Elisabeth Phillips-Smith
Katharine House Hospice, matron

VERSATILE VASES

With a sharp knife, cut around the opaque base of a plastic mineral water bottle. (They come in pretty colours and unblemished with advertising.) Fill it with Oasis (those green absorbent blocks) and arrange available flowers and foliage. It's ideal for a gift (no worry about returning the container!) At Christmas use dried flowers or Christmas decorations.

Rosemary Smith

INVISIBLE SUPPORT

I like to arrange flowers in Oasis but I *don't* like to see it in a cut-glass vase. Instead, I support my arrangements by criss-crossing the top of the vase with clear Sellotape and poking the stems through the gaps. Then the flowers stand up just where I want them.

Tina Simpson
Florist

QUICK FIX

Dried arrangements don't always take kindly to central heating, and anything 'fluffy' can dry out completely and start to shed. Hairspray is an effective treatment, but don't overdo it. Spray just as you would your own hair – that is, all over, evenly, and from a distance of 6–8 inches.

Mrs Anthony Russell

INSTANT POT-POURRI

Making pot-pourri by microwave takes approximately four minutes. Cover a square of absorbent paper with the petals, and put them in the microwave at full power – stopping to turn them once or twice.

The Lady Saye and Sele

DRIED ROSES

You can dry roses most effectively by putting them in a box between layers of cat litter (which can be bought at pet shops and most supermarkets) – and cat owners, don't let your cat use the litter!

Tina Simpson
Florist

SEWING

Everything was finished except just one single cherry-coloured button-hole, and where that button-hole was wanting there was pinned a scrap of paper with these words – in little teeny weeny writing –
NO MORE TWIST.

The Tailor of Gloucester
BEATRIX POTTER

PIN IT

My sewing box was always a tangle of unwound cottons until a tidy-minded friend told me to fix a drawing pin into the top of each reel and wind the thread loosely round it.

Sylvia Winterbottom
Computer programmer

DRAWN UP

A magnet is by far the quickest way to collect up scattered pins.

Margaret Middleditch
Katharine House Hospice, Secretary

DOUBLE TROUBLE

If you want to sew with double thread, knot each thread separately and it won't tangle.

HKH Princess Lillian of Sweden

PIPELINES

Think before you buy piping cord. If it's to be sewn on to silk, choose one with a 'sleeve': these material-covered cords are much kinder to lightweight fabrics. For firmer fabrics, look for a flanged cord: this kind wears well and stays put because it has a piece of fabric attached that can be sewn straight into the seam.

Angela Darling
Interior decorator

BRIDAL VEIL

A fine bridal veil is a lovely heirloom but so easily torn. It can be invisibly mended with patience and loving care using a white hair and a fine needle.

Maureen Buck
Dressmaker

WHY SEW?

When hemming a curtain, why sew? Use Copydex.

Iris Murdoch
Author

AT ARM'S LENGTH

When you want to shorten the sleeves of a coat or jacket – this is especially good for children's clothes – just take a tuck in the lining. There is then no need to cut the material and when you want to let the sleeve down, you just let out the tuck.

Annabel Barnett
Tailoress

NAME TAPES

Sewing name tapes on to socks is my least favourite occupation – and when I had three children away at prep school it seemed almost a full-time job. Eventually I discovered that if I folded each tape in half, putting the short ends together, two or three stitches were enough to hold it in place.

Tarn Dearden
Cash Course organizer

PRESERVING PAPER PATTERNS

Anyone who makes their own clothes will know from bitter experience how fragile paper patterns can be, but spraying them with fabric protector will make them last much longer – and crease less easily too.

Mrs Kenneth Harper

EXPERT INTERLINING

Use cotton to interline the collar, cuffs and facings of a white blouse. Ready-made interlinings tend to 'tint' the fabric once it's been washed, so that it never looks quite clean.

Maria Montes-Riveiro
Spanish daily

PRESS AS YOU GO

I do quite a lot of dressmaking and find it is a lot easier to put the finished garment together if I iron each piece as I go along.

Erica Barnes
Producer, Radio Oxford

SCISSORS THAT NEVER STRAY

I tether my embroidery scissors to my needlework with a length of wool. That way they are always to hand and it discourages the family from borrowing them.

Mrs John Charlton

WOOLS WHERE YOU WANT THEM

I love needlepoint patterns with lots of colours, but my wools get into such a tangle! Now I put each colour into its own little polythene bag, with an inch or two hanging out and a rubber band round its neck. They all sit snugly in my work bag and keep themselves to themselves.

The Lady Wardington

ENSURING A SMOOTH EDGE

Needlepoint canvas not only unravels as you work but catches on your clothes. Bind the edges with masking tape and remove it when the work is finished.

The Hon. Mrs Tyser

NICE TO BE NEAR

To keep wool clean while knitting, put it in a pedal-bin liner and close it with an elastic band so that the wool will run out as you knit. This is very convenient, since you can then place it on the floor next to your seat.

Mrs A. King

SPECIAL OCCASIONS

Party is the madness of many, for the gain of a few.

JONATHAN SWIFT

PLANNING A CHURCH SERVICE

Save the service sheet of every wedding you go to. Then, when it comes to planning one yourself, you have a ready-made selection of hymns etc. to choose from. This works for funerals, too. In fact, it can be even more helpful then, at a time when decisions have to be made quickly and when you are probably too distressed to make them.

The Lord Montagu of Beaulieu

HOUSE SCENTING

When having a party, put a few of drops of essential oils into a bowl of hot water in the hall to make your house inviting to your guests. Choose scents that you like and even mix them: essential oils are available everywhere now, especially in health food shops.

Liza Goddard
Actress

AN IMPROMPTU ARRANGEMENT

When you've been so tied to the kitchen before a dinner party that you come dangerously near to overlooking the flowers, strew the centre of the table with strands of ivy and scatter them with rose petals. If there's time, it's a nice touch to tie each napkin with a strand of ivy, too, and tuck in a rose head.

Jane Packer
Floral designer

LAYING THE TABLE

When setting the table for a dinner party, put the chairs round the table *before*, not *after*, the laying up. It's by far the best way of making sure in advance that there's enough elbow room – and your male guests get the table legs!

Mildred Nash
Parlourmaid

A TALKING POINT

Collecting plates is a fascinating hobby, but unless they are rare or precious it is more fun actually to use them. Unmatched dinner plates can look charming if the colours are harmonious and the patterns in scale, and almost always become a talking point.

The Dowager Marchioness of Reading

THE PERILS OF PLACEMENT

After one never-to-be-forgotten evening when I had jotted down the seating plan for a formal dinner on the back of an old envelope and lost it on the way to the dining-room, a kind friend gave me a placement planner from Asprey's. A cheaper and just as effective method is to write your guests' names on little cards and jiggle them around until you get the seating right. You can then use the same cards as place markers on the table.

The Lady Wardington

NOTHING LEFT TO CHANCE

Only superwomen or the romantic male lead in the movies can whisk up a meal while the guests stand round in the kitchen, glass in hand. In real life the best dinner parties are the ones with the best laid plans. I unashamedly make lists and stick them on the refrigerator door, so that, even after a couple of drinks, I can move through the last-minute routine – 'take salad out of fridge', 'add pine-nuts to casserole', 'melt chocolate sauce', etc. – without having to think. If I omit these pedantic precautions I discover the uneaten salad when I'm washing up, or find the chocolate sauce still frozen while the ice cream is melting fast.

Prue Leith
Restaurateur

THE RIGHT GARNISH

A sprinkling of exactly the right garnish makes all the difference to the appearance of plain foods. Try scattering poppy seeds over savoury pastry crusts ... freshly-milled pepper on pale mayonnaise ... toasted sesame seeds over sprigs of white cauliflower ... a dusting of paprika on a cucumber mousse.

Katie Stewart
Cookery writer

FRAGRANT FINISH

Sugar-frosted rose petals are an enchanting and unusual garnish for a delicately flavoured pudding. Pick a heavily scented rose at the peak of its perfection, separate the petals and coat them in lightly whipped eggwhite. Lay them on kitchen paper and sprinkle them with castor sugar. Leave them to dry, but use them within twenty-four hours.

Carmen Basanti
Spanish cook

INSTANT SOUFFLÉS

Freeze individual soufflés at the moment before you would put them in the oven. Put them straight in the oven from the freezer ten minutes or so before you want to eat them. Very impressive for a dinner party!

The Hon. Mrs Price

CRUMBS!

If the carpet is covered with crumbs after a party you have only yourself to blame. Serve only canapés that can be eaten in one mouthful.

Mrs Hudson
Furniture polish manufacturer

PLENTY OF ICE

When you know you're going to need lots of extra ice-cubes for a party, make them in advance and store them in plastic bags in the freezer. If you squirt them with soda water as you bag them they won't become an iceberg.

Sally O'Sullivan
Editor, Good Housekeping

A STRAIGHT CHOICE

Save yourself a great deal of trouble by offering guests before dinner a straight choice between champagne or orange juice. It costs no more, and is likely to make them better company than gin.

Max Hastings
Editor, The Daily Telegraph

OFFER AN ALTERNATIVE

Strawberries and champagne are traditional fare at Lord's, Ascot and Henley. Cream and sugar will probably be offered as well, but there is a delicious alternative. Pour a little Bordeaux wine over the fruit (no cream or sugar) and enjoy a miraculous transformation from the normal taste.

Ted Dexter
Journalist and cricketer

LOOK AFTER YOUR GUESTS

At a wedding, tell the ushers that throughout the reception they must police the room constantly to see if anyone is alone and not talking to anybody. Weddings can be lonely. Aunt Madge may have emerged from purdah from Edinburgh and not know anybody and need looking after.The bride's mother and father should see that everyone is introduced and as happy as, hopefully, the bride and groom are.

I also think that if you have a sit-down lunch or dinner you should move all the women on two places for each course. It's quite fun and jaunts the whole thing up; also, if some lovely young blood is stuck between Aunt Madge from Edinburgh and Aunt Doris from Cornwall, he may be bored out of his skull and need a break after the smoked salmon.

Jilly Cooper
Writer

NAME DROPPING

When introducing someone to a friend whose name you have forgotten, go ahead and announce the person whose identity is on your lips. The secret is to conduct the exchange with a flourish. 'I want you to meet Jemima Puddleduck, my old flatmate,' you say, without completing the introduction, almost as if it were unnecessary. In the brief pause that follows it is ten to one that the unnamed person will announce themselves.

Drusilla Beyfus
Writer, editor and broadcaster

TAKE A BOX

Even if you think – or have been told – that the theatre is full, find out if there are any free boxes. For some reason people seem to forget about boxes. Anyway, it's worth asking.

Sylvia Lamond
Writer

CHRISTMAS LIGHTS

Save a long, strong cardboard tube that posters come in and after Christmas, when you dismantle the tree, wind the sets of lights very carefully round the tube, pushing them neatly together (I find three sets fit comfortably on to one tube with room to spare). Tuck the ends in and wind the last spare flex tightly to wrap the plugs in firmly. Store the whole thing somewhere out of everyday reach. I have kept my lights without a single breakage in this way for the past twenty-four years.

Susan Hill
Novelist and playwright

PUBLIC SPEAKING

*When I appear in public people expect me to neigh,
grind my teeth, paw the ground and swish my tail –
none of which is easy.*

HRH THE PRINCESS ROYAL

A LAUGH A MINUTE

Informal speaking thrives on humour, not least
because of the confidence if gives you to know
that your next sure-fire winner is never more than
ninety seconds away. Think of them as currants in
a bun – but where to find the currants? The most
reliable jokes and stories are those that have stood
the test of telling, and anyone entertaining the
idea of public speaking really must keep a modest
file marked 'humour' – then pray that Dave Allen
wasn't on television the night before.

Sir Bernard Audley

PUBLIC SPEAKERS PLEASE NOTE

If you don't strike oil in the first five minutes, stop
boring.

The Rt. Rev. Mervyn Stockwood

THE SOUND OF YOUR VOICE

Whenever I have to make a speech (which I hate), I always write it out first, then 'speak' it into a tape recorder. That way I not only get the timing right, but can hear exactly how I'm going to sound to an audience. By listening to yourself you can also tell where the pauses should come, and which words or phrases you need to emphasise to make a point. (You've got a record of what you've said, too, should you ever need to refer to it or, heaven forbid, be invited back.)

Laurie Purden
Journalist

OFF THE CUFF

There is nothing more boring than somebody reading a previously written speech – the temptation of the despairing audience being to count the number of pages yet to be waded through by the speaker. But always write the introduction (and preferably learn it by heart), then have ideas written down as markers and swim between them. And do write the last bit, so that you have something rather well thought out to sit down on.

Hugo Vickers
Biographer

UNACCUSTOMED AS I AM

If you find yourself faced with having to make speeches, remember that, to start with, everyone is nervous. The thing is to gain confidence by actually doing it. Make it easy for yourself by practising on small groups with short speeches on subjects you really know about – your garden, your car, your home. That way you won't have to think about the content, just the delivery.

Another good tip is: say what you are going to say, say it, say what you've said and sit down.

The Rt. Hon. Michael Heseltine
MP

SPEECH-SAVER

If you totally lose your place in the middle of making an important speech, fill the gap by saying, 'The human mind is the most amazing mechanism in the world – it starts to work the moment you are born and only stops when you stand in front of a group of people to make a speech.' One hopes that in the ensuing laughter you will be able to go through your notes and carry on with head held high.

Heard on BBC Radio 4

RAISING MONEY FOR CHARITY

Every little helps, said the ant, pissing into the ocean at midday.

P. GAWDY, 1602

TRY, TRY AGAIN

In my experience the essential thing is to persevere right up to the very end and when, as will invariably happen, the road seems blocked, keep ferreting around looking for every possible opening. Seldom, I find, does one manage a great leap, but the man who keeps moving forward gets there in the end.

Group Captain Leonard Cheshire
Founder of the Cheshire Homes

PERSONAL APPROACH

When raising money for charity, never write a letter if a visit or phone call will do. The more personal the approach, the better the result. This year it helped to produce from £5 to £600,000 per gift for the charities I help.

Ian Kerr
Fundraising consultant

WHAT ARE FRIENDS FOR

A friend is the best person to ask for a donation to a charity, but be sure to ask for enough. To ask for £10,000 when they can only afford £10 is stupid – but to ask for £10 when they could give £10,000 is even more stupid.

Robert Vincent
Accountant

THANK YOU, THANK YOU

Say please and thank you; and having said thank you, say it again in a few months' time and you might have the opportunity of saying thank you again.

Richard Radcliffe
Charities consultant

A CONVIVIAL GATHERING

Invite a fundraising consultant to dinner together with some of your more imaginative friends. Steer the conversation into fund raising. Provide copious amounts of wine. Listen intently. Take surreptitious notes.

Will Eades
Templeton College, Oxford

THE SHORT SHARP BURST

After a dinner or some large and cheerful social function, take out a £5 or £10 note and announce a spontaneous 'fundraiser' for your charity. Write your name on your own note and place it in a box. Urge others to do the same. Mix the notes

thoroughly and draw one, giving whoever signed it
half the kitty. Your charity takes the rest.

Richard Molineux
Fundraising consultant

THE BORE BALL

A charity ball with a difference! Send out
invitations *not* to attend along with the offer of an
exorbitantly priced lapel badge with the logo 'I did
not go to the Bore Ball'. This saves a lot of time
and trouble – and makes a surprising amount of
money.

Peter Panteli
Fundraising consultant

RE-USABLE POSTERS

If you are running a series of events, you will need
publicity. Have some *very* bright posters printed
with the charity's details but leave an A4-sized
blank space in the centre. You can then attach
details of the latest event on handwritten or
photocopied A4 sheets. This is much cheaper than
having posters printed for each event.

Andrew Brackenbury
Fundraising consultant

EMERGENCIES AND DILEMMAS

If you can keep your head when all about you are losing theirs, you don't fully understand the situation.

ANON.

FROZEN REMEDY

We always keep a medium-sized packet of frozen peas available – not to eat, but to act as an instant ice-pack for burns and scalds in the kitchen. This is easier and more flexible than trying to make an ice-pack when the accident happens.

David Lewin
Film critic

MINOR BURNS

If you scald yourself, cut a raw potato in half, scrape its surface with a knife or fork to release the juices, and hold it against the burn for about ten minutes. If applied soon enough, it completely prevents pain and blistering. This is an old Afghan remedy, and really works.

Michael Gurzon

BARBECUED

Should you get burnt at a pool-side barbecue, jump straight into the water. Lots of cold water is the best remedy for even severe burns.

The Lady Wardington

RELIEVING SUNBURN

Applying eggwhite or calamine lotion to sunburnt skin helps to relieve the pain.

Nigel Talbot-Rice
Headmaster of Summerfields

... Painful sunburn can be eased with a paste of milk and bicarbonate of soda.

Joe Pitt
Headmaster, village primary school

CALMING DOWN

The fastest way to take the sting and redness out of sunburnt skin is to apply either a liberal coating of natural yoghurt or to smooth the juice of half a tomato on to the burn. The acid content of either will calm the skin within 6–8 hours.

Alix Kirsta
Health and beauty writer

HARD TO SWALLOW

If a fishbone sticks in your throat, gargle at once with a strong solution of bicarbonate of soda and water.

Nan Stratton

BEE CAUTIOUS

A bee sting is a shaft with a little sac of poison at the top so be very careful how you remove it. Incautious squeezing can force the poison down into the skin – the very thing you want to avoid. Try to *brush* the sting out with gentle strokes. If the top breaks off in the process, then it's quite safe to pull out the remains of the sting.

Colin Franklin
Beekeeper

THE STING

When a huge hornet stung me in Tennessee last summer, my hosts grabbed a cigarette, peeled a little of the paper away from the non-filter end and wet the tobacco. This they pressed on to the sting so that the nicotine juice covered it. It gave almost instant relief!

Mrs David Mackenzie

TENDER

If you are stung by a jellyfish, apply meat tenderizer at once – it will remove the sting and the pain.
P.S. I carry it with me *always* – you never know.

Denholm Elliott
Actor

NUMBER ONE CURE

If you tread on a sea-urchin, the first thing to do is to remove the spiky bit from your foot. The second thing to do – and it really is the only sure way to prevent infection – is to pee on it.

Sir Lees Mayall
Former ambassador to Venezuela

SUCKING UP

If your kitchen is besieged with ants, get out your vacuum cleaner and suck them up. They'll vanish instantly.

Lady Fox

OIL ON TROUBLED WORKS

It's so easy to get into the bath with your watch on, and if it is not waterproof it can be ruined. Save the situation by opening the back and pouring oil – any oil – into the case. This will stop the works rusting and a watch mender will just have to clean it.

Simon Teakle
Christie's jewellery department

SAVE THE SPIDER

When you find an enormous spider sitting in the bath, drape a length of loo paper over the edge so that it is touching the bottom. Leave it there overnight, and the spider will use it as a ladder and be gone by morning – out of sight, anyway!

Lillian Hutton
Housekeeper

IN THE DOG HOUSE

Even the best-behaved dog can sometimes let you down in other people's houses. Spot the puddle quickly enough, though, and no one need be any the wiser if you dowse it with soda water, blot it well in, and then mop up.

Terry Wogan
TV personality

BROKEN BULBS

Should you have the bad luck to break a light bulb while trying to unscrew it, the jagged edges can be very dangerous. Even so, you should be able to ease it out of the socket quite safely if you impale the sharp ends on a bar of soap and cover it with a cloth to get a firm grip.

Ludovic Kennedy
Writer and broadcaster

DENTAL DILEMMAS

If a cap or crown should work loose, try this temporary repair until you can get to a dentist. Chew up some chewing-gum until it's nice and soft and then, after making quite sure that the inside of the cap is dry, wrap a smidgen of gum around it. Press the cap firmly back on to the tooth and the gum will hold it in place for the time being.

If (worse) you lose a cap altogether and have to appear in public, white chewing gum moulded into a tooth shape round the stump will hide the gap until help is at hand.

Donald Derrick
Dental surgeon

THE HAND BAG

Have you noticed that you only have to get up to the elbows in dough or some such for the telephone to ring? Keep a plastic bag near by so that you can slip your hand into it when you hear the bell.

Hermione Courage
Racehorse owner and breeder

MAKING AN EXIT

If you find yourself in the middle of the first act of an unbearably boring play which you are certain will never improve, clap your handkerchief to your nose and, muttering 'Please excuse me', make your way to the exit. Nobody can be expected to sit through anything with a bad nosebleed.

I cannot claim this as an original hint. This advice was given to me by the late Sir Noel Coward half a century ago and it has proved extremely useful on several occasions since!

Sir John Mills
Actor

TINT STAINS

If your hairdresser tints your skin along with your hair, dry cigarette ash, rubbed quickly into the stain, will remove it.

Kathy O'Shea
Hairstylist at Equus

NO PROBLEM

When I find myself talking to somebody with whom I know I've previously had an intimate conversation but can't for the life of me remember what it was about, I lean towards them in a confidential way and say in a low voice, 'How's the old problem going?' It quite often does the trick.

Neil Gadsby
Katharine House Hospice Trust, chairman

HOT AND COLD

To separate two glasses that have stuck together, one inside the other, fill the inside one with cold water, then put them both in hot water.

Clifford Smart
Barman

OPENING STUBBORN BOTTLES

Sometimes it seems almost impossible to open a wide-necked vacuum-sealed bottle of tomato or fruit juice. Turn it upside down and tap the lid smartly on the floor. This will break the vacuum and it will unscrew easily.

The Hon. Mrs Sergison-Brooke

THE RIGHT AMOUNT

How to coax tomato sauce out of its bottle – that is the question. You'll be tempting fate if you up-end the bottle over your plate and slap its bottom. The trick is to give it a really good shake-up first – with the lid on.

Wallace Reyburn
Writer

… Take great care when you shake the bottle, first none will come and then a lot'll.

Anon.

ZIPPING UP

There's nothing more infuriating than a zip that won't zip. I unstick mine by rubbing them up and down with the moistened end of a bar of soap.

Lady Georgina Coleridge
Journalist and writer

An ordinary lead pencil run up and down both sides of that ever-troublesome zip fastener will free it immediately – it's the graphite that does it.

Giles
Cartoonist

DRIP-DRIP-DRIP

If the sound of a dripping tap in the middle of the night is driving you wild and you can't raise a plumber until morning, hang a piece of string from the tap to plughole so that the drips slide down it without plopping.

Sir Allan Green

INSTANT HEMMING

If you catch your heel in your hem just as you are going out, double-sided sticky tape does a wonderful instant-repair job.

Angela Uzielli
Ladies Open Golf Champion 1990

COLD FEET

To keep your feet warm in very cold weather, use Thermogene, cut to size, to make inner soles for your gumboots.

Mrs Francis Sitwell

HOT NEWS

Don't laugh – but wrapping yourself up in newspaper on a train without heating is just as effective as wearing thermal underwear.

The Hon. Mrs James Ogilvy

OOPS!

Nothing is more pervasive than the smell of sick. It's almost impossible, for instance, to get it out of a car. But if you sprinkle bicarbonate of soda on the place as soon as you have mopped it up, there won't be a whiff in the morning.

Mrs Douglas Wise

CAN'T FIND IT?

If you have lost something and it is not quickly found, don't rush around looking in all sorts of impossible places. Sit down and think through where you last had it and where it might be. If you don't know when it was lost, start by assuming that it was only shortly before you noticed that it was gone.

Sir Jeremy Morse
Chairman, Lloyds Bank

DO NOTHING

Advice to all those under contract who suspect that they are about to get the sack: never resign, wait to be fired.

Drusilla Beyfus
Writer, editor and broadcaster

ONE PIECE OF PAPER

In our industry I find that it is only when one can reduce the main points of a complex subject on to one piece of paper that one begins to find the right solutions. This is probably also true of all of us in our own personal affairs.

Simon R. Foster
The Society of Motor Manufacturers and Traders

THE BRAVE START

You face a pile of paperwork on your desk. The temptation is to clear up the easy items first, pushing the more complex ones to the bottom. Try it the other way round, tackle the difficult things first, then you will work up a great momentum for the rest.

The Lord Prentice

DECISION-MAKING

The best labour-saving scheme I discovered as Bishop of Liverpool and subsequently as Archbishop of York was to have a file marked 'Too Difficult', dealing with matters which, in the nature of things, could never be solved or would solve themselves without human contrivance. It saved a lot of meaningless effort and unnecessary qualms of conscience. Thoroughly recommended to hard-pressed executives.

Lord Blanch

MORE DECISION-MAKING

When you are fretting around, worrying about moving house, losing your job, getting married or setting up in business, just tell yourself: 'Big decisions make themselves', so don't exhaust yourself with 'what if' scenarios.

Louise Botting
Presenter, Money Box

THANK GOD

Instead of listing your sins and telling God you are sorry for them, thank Him for all your successes: diseases you did not catch, and the things you did right. A bar of nut-milk chocolate makes a good amen!

Rabbi Lionel Blue

THE ELEVENTH COMMANDMENT

Thou shalt not be found out.

Sir Jimmy Savile
TV and radio presenter

THINKING AHEAD
It takes time to save time.

JOE TAYLOR

A BOX OF CARDS

Whenever I see a card I like (for birthdays,
anniversaries and so on) I buy it and put it in a
box. The family raid the collection ruthlessly and I
have to keep topping it up, but it does save a great
many unnecessary trips to the shops.

Mrs Tony Slater

MESSAGES

Instead of leaving telephone messages for other
members of the family on scraps of paper and
backs of envelopes, buy a large, brightly coloured
hardback notebook and write them all down in it.
You've no idea how often this saves a desperate
hunt for the old newspaper you left the vital
number on. If you're like me you'll probably tend
to lose the notebook as well, but at least it's more
likely to turn up eventually.

Jane Asher
Actress

FINE TUNING

At the risk of seeming extravagant I have three wirelesses, one tuned to each of Radio Two, Three and Four, as this saves a great deal of time fiddling about with the dial.

The Duke of Devonshire

WHERE THERE'S A WILL

The one certainty in this uncertain world is that we are all going to die, so *make a will*. But do see a solicitor to make sure not only that it is valid but that your intentions are clear: any ambiguity can lead at best to uncertainty and at worst to expensive litigation. (In one noted case a man said on a will form that he left 'all to Mother', which sounded straightforward enough until a girlfriend appeared from the wings claiming that he always called her 'Mother' too.) It is also important to update one's will if there is any change in family circumstances – and to keep it where it can easily be found.

Tony Baldry
MP

NEVER SAY OI!

Taxi drivers are much more sensitive than you think. I never stop for anyone who whistles, or shouts OI! – *never*, nor do any of my mates. The best way to get a cab when it's raining is to stay in the same place, don't keep darting about, and hold up your hand so that you can be seen clearly.

London cabbie

… I find I can always get a taxi when I'm wearing a hat.

Mrs Robert Dean

INSPIRATION

Advice received on how to write a book: always use plenty of paper and never do less than ten minutes a day.

Lady Selina Hastings
Author

GOING FOR A SONG

If you're looking for a bargain, go to a Metropolitan Police auction. Every month or so they sell off stolen goods through a firm of London auctioneers. I got a really good bike for a fraction of the price of a new one, but they have plenty of other things as well, like cameras, car cassettes and stereos, golf clubs, typewriters – even computers. It's up to you, though, to make sure they work.

Julian Soper
Student

UPSTAIRS, DOWNSTAIRS

Before your guests arrive, put a generous dash of bath essence in the downstairs loo to make the cloakroom smell as nice as the bathrooms.

Derek Collins
Accommodation agent

PET OWNERS' SOLACE

When dog owners come to stay it's not a bad idea to put a bottle of soda water in their bedrooms (they're sure to know that soda water deals with embarrassing puddles) – and a small carafe of whisky to calm their nerves.

The Lord Grantley

THOUGHTFUL TOUCHES

Some house guests, particularly if they are no longer young, don't like to appear to be a nuisance, so you should think ahead about what might please them to find in their room. Books and magazines certainly – the elderly tend to be wakeful. But also, perhaps, mineral water and biscuits – even an electric kettle and some teabags etc. so that they can make a hot drink if they want to, without having to ask for it.

Mrs John Treneman

A LITTLE OF WHAT THEY FANCY

Keep a record of your guest's dietary problems. These days so many people are either watching their weight, or have to cut out certain foods for health reasons, that an easy-to-refer-to record is essential if you want to avoid the last-minute preparation of something suitable – and your guest's embarrassment at having to ask for it.

Anon.

BOOKING A TABLE

You get a better table in a restaurant if you book one for four people, even if there are only three of you. When you are seated you apologize profusely to the maître and explain that the fourth member of your party has been detained and may not arrive.

Eden Phillips
Publishing director

WAKEY WAKEY

Some people just can't wake up. Putting the alarm

clock on a tin plate can double its sound and
might do the trick.

Paul Hayter
Reading clerk, House of Lords

HOME VIDEO

It can happen that six months after a burglary you
realize that some treasured knick-knack has gone,
and it is too late to claim on the insurance. Be
prepared by making a video of your home – borrow
or hire a camera if necessary – and wander from
room to room, zooming in on all ornaments and
pictures. For a complete record you can make a
running commentary at the same time.

The Lord Wardington

KEEPING A RECORD

If you collect pictures, make the time to
photograph them (any ordinary camera will do)
and note down the name of the artist, the year
painted, and so on. Should you be unlucky enough
to be burgled, the police and your insurance
company will want to know exactly what you've
lost – and a photograph speeds things along.

Laurie Purden
Journalist

LOCK PICKING

Never have your letter-box at the same level as
your front door lock. It's all too easy for a potential
burglar to slip his hand – or, say, a wire coat
hanger – through the opening and pull back the
lock handle, particularly if it is the lever kind.

Patricia Lamburn
Area co-ordinator, Neighbourhood Watch

HIDDEN ASSETS

Hide a £10 note – or more if you can spare it – somewhere in your car. In that ghastly moment when you're stranded without your wallet or cheque book, it can be a lifesaver.

The Hon. John Hesketh

SOCK IT TO 'EM

Keep a few odd socks in the boot of the car. When you've been shopping, put bottles in them to stop them from banging together.

Katie Boyle
TV and radio personality

POUND SAVER

Always pay your bills by the bank giro system rather than posting them. A short walk down the high street once a month can save pounds. Also, if possible, never make phone calls between 9 a.m. and 1.00 p.m. because it is much cheaper at other times.

Margaret Allen
Financial journalist

TEMPTATION

Never go shopping when you're hungry. You end up buying lots of little delicacies with the same sell-by date and eventually slinging most of them out.

Alice Thomas Ellis
Writer

LET YOUR FINGERS DO THE WALKING

Write your shopping list in the order in which it

can be accomplished with the least walking. It
saves time and energy and you won't forget things.

Noelle Walsh

TIME MANAGEMENT

When writing a list of tasks for the following
day/week, write them in order of importance. Make
sure you do the first thing first – and finish it.

Sue Warner
Charity adviser

MAKING NOTES

Make a note of anything that occurs to you –
never trust your memory because you will
invariably forget.

Christina Foyle
Founder, Foyle's Literary Luncheons

WORDS TO THE WISE

Always get it in writing, but never write anything
down.

Frankie McGowan
Journalist

THE EASY WAY OUT

My idea of a good idea is to get someone else to
do it for me!

Patric Walker
Astrologer

PENNY WISE

Look after your pennies and the pounds will look
after themselves.

Willie Carson
Champion jockey

PRESENTS

Why is it no one ever sent me yet
One perfect limousine, do you suppose?
Ah no, it's always just my luck to get
One perfect rose.

DOROTHY PARKER

THE GREEDY BOOK

My mother-in-law introduced me to the Greedy
Book. It's a marvellous way of finding out what each
member of the family wants for Christmas (or
birthdays, or whatever). All you do is provide a
large, hard-backed notebook, and allot each person
their own page. Then throughout the year they can
write down all the things they'd like most, from a set
of pencils to a Porsche. It doesn't mean they'll
actually get them, of course, but even the fantasies
are fun – and make amusing reading in later years.

The Lady Wardington

GIVE AS YOU GET

I like to give (and to get) the kind of things you
never think of buying for yourself – like really
beautiful padded hangers.

Nanette Newman
Actress and author

KEY TO SUCCESS

I always find it difficult to think of presents for children, having none of my own. A good idea I find is to buy a piggy bank or any old secondhand coin box and fill it with as many coins as you choose to put in, or can afford. You can give the key to the child or the parents as you see fit, though I've always found it more successful to give it to the child concerned.

Carmen Callil
Publisher

THE GIFT OF KNOWLEDGE

Give children (and grandchildren) a secondhand set – ten volumes – of Arthur Mee's old *Children's Encyclopaedia*. Its science and politics are seventy years out of date, but it remains the best and most painless introduction to poetry, art, nature; history, folklore, and indeed all that makes for a civilized education.

George MacDonald Fraser
Author and journalist

A PLOT OF YOUR OWN

For our daughter's eighteenth birthday we gave her a six-foot square plot of land in Wales, planted with a young oak. It's part of a scheme by Heritage Conserved (Afallon, High Street, Llanfyllin, Powys) to create a wood which, because the land is collectively owned, and can't be developed, will be there for ever. Each plot and the tree of your choice costs £17.50. They then send you deeds, and look after the tree for five years, until it's well established.

Mrs John Colwell

STARTING A SET

China is an ideal godparent present. You give part of a set – as much as you like – at the time of the christening, and then a plate (or whatever) each birthday until the set is complete. You can do the same thing with glasses, which is probably better if it's a boy.

The Hon. Mrs James Ogilvy

FIFTY GLORIOUS YEARS

Golden weddings are such wonderful occasions but what do you give the happy couple? Fifty yellow roses? Not a bad idea.

Lady Helen Smith

ON THE MAT

Weekending with a multi-millionaire not long ago, I was stuck to think of an original but inexpensive present to give someone who has everything money can buy. So I photographed him and his dog on the terrace, took the negative along to Boots who translated it into some very attractive, felt-backed table mats. They make coasters, too. My host was delighted and has to be restrained from using them for formal dinner parties.

Joyce Hopkirk
Journalist

THE WHAT-TO-TAKE PROBLEM

Taking your hostess cut flowers is *not* a good idea. She will already have her own and won't have time to arrange them. Candles are the perfect present – and one can never have too many.

Michael Graham
Hotelier

WITHIN REACH

For someone in hospital, fill a small basket with a handle with brush, comb, mirror, pen, small pad, tissues and/or other small items you think they'll need. Leave it on the bedside table, so they can reach the whole basket and select what they want without having to ask for help.

Felicity Kendal
Actress

PASS GO

Foreign versions of Monopoly are fun. I like playing with the Champs Elysées one week, Fifth Avenue the next, and I often bring sets home with me from abroad to give as presents.

David Shilling
Hat designer

NO NEED TO ASK

Ask your mother-in-law for a dishwasher. I didn't have to ask: bless her, she took one look at me and gave us hers.

Edwina Currie
MP

THE GRAB BAG

An attractive way to provide presents for everyone at a party – and more rewarding than most crackers – is to make a Grab Bag. Wrap up little presents, tie a long coloured ribbon to each (possibly pink for girls, blue for boys) and pile them into a basket with the ends hanging out. At a given moment, each guest picks up a ribbon and pulls.

Ioanna Malone
Translator

GIFT TAGS GALORE

A money-saving idea for making gift tags is to cut out the pretty bits from old Christmas and birthday cards (a robin, say, or a flower), punch a hole in one corner and thread through a bright ribbon. Make sure, though, that there's nothing written on the back!

Mrs Kenneth Harper

IN THE NEWS

Christmas presents wrapped in newspaper and tied with scarlet ribbon look very effective, and it's amusing to choose whichever newspaper matches the recipient's political persuasion. But I always double-wrap the newspaper in cellophane first – the shiny kind that florists use. This takes more time, of course, but it then looks really special – and the cellophane stops the print from rubbing off on your fingers.

Roland Klein
Fashion designer

THE PERFECT PRESENT

Books make perfect presents, and what better than a copy of *Superhints*? But don't give them this one, buy another. Remember, all the royalties go to the Katharine House Hospice.

The Lady Wardington

INDEX OF HINTS

INDEX OF NAMES